For Barbara and Dennis
best as always
Paul
'86

The Language Parallax

Texas Linguistics Series

Editorial Board

The Language Parallax *By Paul Friedrich*

Linguistic Relativism
and Poetic
Indeterminacy

University of Texas Press   Austin

First edition, 1986

Requests for permission to reproduce material from this work should be
sent to:
  Permissions
  University of Texas Press
  Box 7819
  Austin, Texas 78713

Library of Congress Cataloging-in-Publication Data

Friedrich, Paul, 1927–
  The language parallax.

  (Texas linguistics series)
  Bibliography: p.
  Includes index.
  1. Sapir-Whorf hypothesis. 2. Poetry. 3. Languages
—Philosophy. I. Title. II. Series.
PS35.F72 1986   306'.4   85-15091
ISBN 0-292-74650-4
ISBN 0-292-74651-2 (pbk.)

See pages 181–182 for permission notices.

For my mother, Lenore Friedrich,
my daughter, Kanya,
and my wife, Deborah

Contents

Figures

Tables

Paul Friedrich:
An Appreciation

I first became acquainted with the name of Paul Friedrich when I read his brilliant review (in *Language* 37 : 163 – 168, 1961) of the volume *Linguistic Diversity in South Asia*, edited by Charles Ferguson and John Gumperz. Apart from his appropriate criticism of the papers (including mine), I was especially impressed by his delightful term "orthographic dazzle"—referring to the effect that a prestigious writing system can have on literate speakers' consciousness of their language. Subsequently, I enjoyed reading Paul's 1962 articles, "Language and Politics in India" and "An Evolutionary Sketch of Russian Kinship"; and in 1964 I had the pleasure of meeting him for the first time at the UCLA Sociolinguistics Conference in Los Angeles and at Arrowhead Lake. I still have a strong visual and auditory memory of Paul's paper, "Structural Implications of Russian Pronominal Usage." His effective recitation of extended passages from Gorki, Gogol, Tolstoy, Dostoyevsky, and Pushkin—as well as his sensitive analysis of those authors' usage of pronouns—moved his audience to an ovation. I might have guessed then that Paul was at heart not only an anthropologist and linguist, but a poet as well.

In the following years, we remained in touch, mainly through correspondence concerning several manuscripts—especially on the Tarascan language—which I accepted from Paul in my capacity as editor of *Language*. I came to know him as a scholar of extraordinary range, whose competence was displayed by now-classic works in such diverse fields as political anthropology (*Agrarian Revolt in a*

Mexican Village, 1977), comparative Indo-European (*Proto-Indo-European Trees,* 1970), and theory of verbal aspect (*On Aspect Theory and Homeric Aspect,* 1974). I also appreciated the geographical breadth of his interests, which include South Asia, Mexico, Russia, ancient Greece, and indeed the whole Proto-Indo-European world.

More recently, however, even further aspects of Paul's creativity were revealed to me by his *Meaning of Aphrodite* (1978)—a study of myth which is at once philological, anthropological, and poetic— and by his *samizdat* collections of poems, *Neighboring Leaves Ride This Wind* (1976) and *Bastard Moons* (1979b).

When a volume of my own collected papers was published in 1976, Paul reviewed it for *Language* (1978); but at the suggestion of a similar collection of his own papers, to be edited by A. Dil, Paul wrote me that he was "not yet ready to be pickled." Fortunately he relented, and in 1979 his book *Language, Context, and the Imagination* was published. The title of the volume, taken as the conjunction of three terms (never a disjunction!), clearly indicates the thrust of Paul's work. Along with twelve reprinted articles, that volume also included the essay "Poetic Language and the Imagination," which previously had received only limited distribution; here he began explicitly to discuss poetic creativity as a key factor in understanding the nature and use of language. A revised version of that essay forms Chapter 3 of the present volume.

What I have written above has been largely in terms of personal interaction. This is because of my own feeling that understanding of human existence in general can often be best reached through consideration of individual experience—a view which is also apparent in much of Paul's work, e.g., his studies of the Tarascan leader Primo Tapia and the Homeric hero Achilles, and in the intensely personal nature of many of his poems. I will not attempt to paraphrase here the broader insights into "language, context, and the imagination" which Paul offers in the essays that follow. I will only say that, in combining the gift for rigorous, explicit analysis of linguistic facts with a suitable appreciation of the "order-to-chaos continuum" in language, Paul reminds me of no one so much as that other prolific anthropologist-linguist-poet, Edward Sapir. I've always regretted that I was born too late to know Sapir; but I'm delighted that I know Paul Friedrich.

William Bright

Acknowledgments

For their comments on various versions of various portions of THE LANGUAGE PARALLAX I am particularly indebted to John Attinasi and Dell Hymes, who critiqued three chapters each (3, 4, and 7, and 2, 3, and 6, respectively); Joel Sherzer on chapter 2; Margaret Egnor, David Price, Joel Sherzer, and Roy Wagner on chapter 3 (of the earlier, unfinished version of 1979 [pp. 441–513], where full personal and bibliographical acknowledgments are listed); otherwise, Steve Caton on the present version, which was essentially constituted by fall 1982 (with the later addition of "Industrial Accident: Mexico"); the '70s research in chapter 4 benefited from Margaret Hardin, Max and Lisa Lethrop, and Michael Silverstein; chapter 5 from Ray Fogelson, Linn Hart, John Leavitt, Paul Liffman, Bruce Mannheim, Milton Singer, and Bonnie Urciuoli (it was written on the encouragement of Kenneth Atchity of *Dreamworks*); David Bevington, Françoise Meltzer, Donna Jo Napoli, Robert von Hallberg, and Lisa Crone on chapter 6; William Bright, Margaret Egnor, and A. K. Ramanujan on poems allied to chapter 7; James Birdsell, Ranjit Chatterjee, Ray Fogelson, Paul Liffman, James Lindholm, Alexis Manaster-Ramer, Tony Woodbury, and Roy Wagner on chapter 8 (simplified considerably in matters of bibliographical reference from the 1980 version); and finally, Steve Tyler on chapter 9. The translation from Dante on p. 121 was synthesized from Ciardi, Norton, and Bickerton. Ivan Brady, on the basis of two of these chapters, encouraged me at an early stage, and I remain grateful to him for this. Anwar Dil, learned linguist and poet, provided a crucial metaphor years ago.

Speaking more comprehensively, Tim Buckley must be singled out for critiquing all but chapters 4 and 6. Christine Gever did a superb editing job on the manuscript, as did Gail Hajenian Miller on the index. Above all, I am grateful to my wife Deborah Gordon Friedrich, who contributed to the style, organization, and overall ideas in this book at all levels of all chapters and staunchly supported the whole enterprise.

P.F.

Chicago   1985

The Language Parallax

parallax, n. 1. the apparent change in the position of an object resulting from a change in the direction or position from which it is viewed.

Webster's New Twentieth Century Dictionary

Introduction

In a sense that is simple but pertinent, linguistic relativism and the closely related linguistic chauvinism are forms of awareness that have been evolving among us for a long time. They must have been acute in the Upper Paleolithic, when Cro-Magnons ordered their enmities and mobilized their affinities on the basis, in part, of how families "over there" spoke. Linguistic chauvinism was endemic in early Greek thought, and in Greek philosophy the dispute over "nature versus convention" constitutes an integral part of what might be called proto-relativism (since "convention" is language-culture specific). The Age of Discovery and subsequent Colonialism enormously stimulated speculation both on differences between languages and their relative qualities and on the dialectically related question of what might be common or universal. A cultivated relativism certainly was essential to Romanticism, in both its literary and its national and folkloristic phases. And relativism in more sophisticated senses has received much critical and scientific attention over the past hundred years, to the degree that a great deal of anthropology and linguistics can be interpreted as input—if often implicitly or unwittingly. There is an obvious, dialectical relation between relativism and chauvinism, ethnocentrism, and racism, just as relativism may contribute to international understanding, political pluralism, and even cross-language poetic inspiration; in short, relativism has powerful political, ethical, and aesthetic implications. Some of these are expressed below in terms of outrage against exploitation, and guilt about ethnic conflict. Otherwise, the present volume draws on the culture history alluded to above and on the major thinkers on linguistic relativism (discussed in chapter 2) in order to elaborate a general but in some ways novel version of linguistic relativism and the related hypothesis of poetic indeterminacy.

It is, in fact, through the way it develops the concept of indeterminacy that this new version differs from earlier formulations. The background for such indeterminacy is determinacy: the ubiquitous emphasis in linguistics and other sciences on system and structure, a partly hypothetical universe of ordered rules and arguments and of ordered change involving sets of demarcated classes. The present argument is not opposed to this determinism, nor does it invite a mystical leap into antistructure. Rather, it recognizes the beauty and reality of structure, rule, and other shapes knowable through science; linguistic relativism, in fact, is predicated on some assumption of structure in language and the differences between such structures. But much of the vital process of language involves phenomena beyond the (relatively) minimal features of grammar, logical syntax, or similar things. The present argument presupposes this variable, unpredictable, and dynamic zone, and assumes, in part, that the emotions and motives and even the cognitive world of a human being are significantly beyond the scope of exhaustive description and accurate prediction. I have called this indeterminacy "poetic" (1979a : 498) because so much of it includes phenomena that are usually labeled in this way. The present formulation seeks a balance between the (relativist) determinacy of structure and the (poetic) indeterminacy of the individual who participates in that structure actively and passively.

Let us approach the problem in another way. The basic idea is that the individual in politics, the scientist in the laboratory, and the poet within a tradition and a subculture are all parts of their respective contexts in an interdependency that is symbiotic and reciprocal. Thus the poet is part of a whole, a figure in the great centers of a tradition and to his or her contemporaries who write or at least read poetry. But this tradition and these contemporaries similarly impinge upon and contribute to what Stevens called the "august imagination" and the "squamous mind" of the individual.

My emphasis on imagination and indeterminacy is not meant to imply alienation and solipsism. On the contrary, the individual imagination grows and is nurtured in dialogue with others and is registered in discourse involving pluralities. But discourse and dialogue are not more important or interesting than the participant imagination. The imagination of the unique individual gains particular relevance in the case of poetic language, where the role of the poet or the poetic speaker is more important than the role of the anonymous individual in language structure or the history of language.

The concepts of individual and poetic indeterminacy owe much to the formative theorists of Romanticism, who emphasized individual consciousness in opposition to society and culture. They also emphasized the role of poetic truth in relation to scientific truth. Indeterminacy owes almost as much to the natural science philosophers of this century, particularly physicists such as Heisenberg, and, finally, to a long line of philosophers, poets, and writers about literature such as Nietzsche, Bergson, and Wallace Stevens, all of whom gave adequate scope to the indeterminate. Poetic and individual indeterminacy were dealt with in an original way by Sapir and Cassirer but never given the explicit role that they merited in an overall formulation.

Let us turn to the specific organization of this book. Following a brief intellectual history of linguistic relativism in chapter 2, I argue that the most interesting and surely the most complex differences between natural languages are centered in the relatively poetic levels of sound and meaning, be this poetry strictly speaking or a poetic stratum in other kinds of discourse. I develop this poetic version of the relativism hypothesis in terms of basic premises about continuousness and beauty—for example, figures and tropes ("culture as a work of art")—and then follows a long illustrative discussion of the poetic potential of the Tarascan (pronounced Ta-rás-can) language (with poems of my own about [and through the symbolism of] Tarascan language-culture or simply drawn from, that is, distilled from, Tarascan symbolism). The most basic of these premises is that "the master trope" that makes poetry consists in integrating or organically fusing the music of language with the nuance of myth. The adamant contention that the locus and focus of interlinguistic differences is in poetic language was originally championed by Vico but has been elaborated since by Cassirer, Sapir, and others into a general position.

A special problem within the initial argument for linguistic relativism and poetic indeterminacy is posed by the millennial status of the metaphor. Here the metaphor is alleged to be not only the master trope but the most essential or diagnostic feature of poetry itself and therefore, implicitly, of interlanguage differences. My feeling is that the metaphor is only one subcategory among several classes of figures of speech or, more comprehensively, what in chapter 5 I call *poiesemes* (whatever makes speech and language poetic). The metaphor is only one kind of analogy and part of a much larger context of analogical devices and associational thinking; poetic metaphor should not be confused with analogy in general, or, if one term is needed for both phenomena, then two more should be coined for the more specific domains. My objective is to move toward a more realistic and less ethnocentric point of view.

While poems and similar poetic phenomena are an obvious resource for statements on indeterminacy, indeterminacy also typifies linguistic analysis, including, or perhaps particularly including, linguistic fieldwork. As a supplement to the overall argument of the book, chapter 4 describes some dialectological fieldwork. Following Heisenberg and Whitehead, and contrary to Jakobson and many contemporaries, I think that we must include the observer as part of the field of observation. Actually, there are several observers, or points of view, to be taken into account: the linguistic observer, the speakers whom he/she is observing, and what might be called "the eyes of the text."

To explore these issues of indeterminacy more deeply I then turn to two mutually supplementary, empirical problems: the language of dreams in chapter 5, and the language of sonnets in chapter 6. Dreams most closely adjoin the apparently chaotic world of the unconscious. But we also find that dreams are to a large extent built in a structured way with regular units, definable process, and a higher determinate connection with "the real world." This is illustrated by an in-depth analysis of an actual dream that raises questions about the poetry of dreams and the reference in them to political and economic power. Sonnets, on the other hand, must number among the most structured and, in most hands, fossilized of all linguistic forms, and hence would seem to exemplify linguistic determinism to an extreme degree. Yet closer examination shows that sonnets are open to infinite variation and have evolved recently in the direction of greater anomie in form. Dreams and sonnets illustrate in almost diametrically different ways how the imagination can integrate reality through a poetic language and confront the chaos within itself and in relationships with other persons, as well as in the external worlds of nature, economics, society, and politics. Dreams and sonnets each constitute a kind of limiting case for the general theory.

To take the reader into the center of the problem, there follows a chapter of "poems as parallactic positions." The poems presented exemplify such central issues as the poetry of conversation, the development of common understandings between culturally distinct individuals, the poetic condensation of archaic cultural symbols, and the "love struggle" with language that is integral to growing up, to adjusting to a foreign culture, and to writing poetry in any language. While these poems are obviously "about" issues dealt with elsewhere in this book, they are also about the language in which they are cast, and in some cases about the metalanguages for discussing those languages (e.g., "Proto-Indo-European kinship" is to some extent about Proto-Indo-European linguistics as well as about the reconstructed linguistic symbolism of the Proto-Indo-Europeans). The medium of poetry can enable one to simultaneously constellate personal and general, subjective and objective statements in order to handle situations or realities that are simply too subtle or complicated or multidimensional to be dealt with succinctly in any other way; in brief, one job that a poem often can do better than a discursive statement is to distill gist. Chapter 7, with its poems, complements chapter 4, in which the reader is taken into the situation of a linguist grappling with an almost insuperable problem of dialectal variation and sociolinguistic indeterminacy.

My final general point is to qualify and criticize the assumption that there is a homogeneous or in some sense perfect order underlying language—and all culture. This assumption is revealed with clarity by those anthropologists and linguists who present their field data as particularly problematical or even mysterious, only to then apply our methods and models to emerge with a solution that rationalizes the entire situation. Without belittling their discoveries—in fact, while working in other contexts (such as chapter 4 below) to achieve them myself—I also feel that their rhetoric must be exposed and that, more important, the theory of linguistic relativism must be moved into the late twentieth century. In other words, it must be cast in terms of a synthetic model that comprises order, structure, cause, and teleonomy—because all of these clearly have much truth value—and, on the other hand, the more skeptical and realistic terms that envisage disorder, unpredictability, and an underlying reality that is at least partly chaotic. The indeterminacy of individual speech and of the individual speaker, particularly the poet, is a link between the ascertainable order in language and the intimations of disorder in and beyond language, be it the language of the religious visionary or that of the person of practical action. Unless we find out a great deal that contradicts what we know now about the brain, we will have to assume that words and sentences are to some extent dredged up out of chaos. This is not a matter of some deep, romanticized womb or wellspring, but of degrees of determinacy, predictability, and probability and a partial lack of order at all levels and in all crannies of life that is one of life's hardest and most irreducible facts. The notion of an "order-to-chaos continuum" is elaborated in chapter 8, before a final chapter that sets forth some general goals and prospects.

A more specific goal of this book is to enlarge and in some ways to criticize the positions of the two scholars with whom linguistic relativism is mainly associated: Sapir and Whorf. I value Whorf's massive contribution in popularizing the subject, in relating the theory of relativism to the natural sciences of his day and to fascinating (if usually anecdotal) evidence from American Indian languages, and for generally sharpening the issues with an almost hallucinatory theoretical clarity; in his writings there is a beautiful integration of reason and intuition. I also appreciate the fact that in his remarkable, posthumously published article he moved very far toward a more pragmatic, action- and event-based position (consonant with shifting to semantically complex examples from American English). But I think that his writings must be criticized for their scientism, the occasional misuse of theory from the natural sciences, an overemphasis on morphology and structure in Amerind (as against acts of discourse), and his almost total neglect of the unique individual.

Similarly, I appreciate Sapir's virtues in stating linguistic relativism: his attention to poetic technique, to cultural context, to the role of music, and to the sentient individual, as well as the many other powerful components of what is still the most adequate, comprehensive, and sensitive view of language that has ever been formulated. Some of his points—for example, on language "drift" and how "grammars leak"—are congruous with what I argue below on degrees of order in language. But I disagree with Sapir's occasional elitism (e.g., his condemnation of Whitman in a review of Dickinson), with the way he ignores the role of mendacity and illusion in language in favor of a generically idealistic and Romantic position, and with the way he ignores economic exploitation, colonialism, and the hard facts of power and revolt that should be clearly recognized in any theory of language.

My own general position on linguistic relativism and poetic indeterminacy owes much to the anthropological linguistics of Boas,

Sapir, and Whorf, and the antecedent matrix of eighteenth- and nineteenth-century German humanism (Herder, Goethe). But in a deeper sense I am indebted to the Pascal-to-Camus line of existentialist thought; to Herman Melville and his ideas about chaos and ethics; to Emerson and Wallace Stevens and their peculiarly American position on poetic language, reality, and the imagination (which figures far more in Whorf than is recognized); to Tolstoy (and implicitly Rousseau) and his concern with the individual and with emotional processes; to recent American poetics and to some of the work of the Prague School, particularly Jakobson and Mathesius; and to theorists of modern science, both classical ones such as Heisenberg (indeterminacy) and Whitehead ("structure-in-process") and recent philosophers such as Capra. From these and probably other sources that I cannot recapture I have tried to synthesize a view of several phenomena and their interrelations.

2

A Background History of Linguistic Relativism

INTRODUCTION: THE ORIGINATORS

To the extent that there was an originator or "unique beginner" (and no idea starts from scratch), it was the brilliant and prolific Italian humanist Giambattista Vico (1668–1774). Reacting against the post-Cartesian rationalism of his day, he pioneered in emphasizing the role of history and poetry and, more particularly, the histories of individual peoples and civilizations; within the latter the most distinctive components were myth and language; language was pervasively poetic; to some extent it *was* poetry (just as Frost was to say that all language, except mathematics, is metaphorical). With language seen in this highly poetic way, it is obviously the poet who distills its more subtle features and gives to the myths of a people their linguistically essential expression. Thus, at the dawn of an explicit and elaborated (if not very systematic) linguistic relativism we already find crystallized an ideological/theoretical opposition that closely resembles that of the last two decades: just as Descartes argued for a rationalistic and universalistic point of view, so Vico propugned the emotional, the aesthetic, the historical, and the unique.

The next major contributor, Immanuel Kant (1724–1804), although a titan of the Age of Reason, was also the architect of a more complex reaction against extreme Cartesian rationalism. He clarified the categorical nature of the knowing mind (still a central issue in anthropological linguistics today), and, in one of his earliest and most fundamental books, explored many issues in poetic aesthetics, particularly the problem of "the sublime." A pioneer in the study of anthropology and the first ever to offer a course by that name, he formulated the essence of the middle-of-the-road position that we also associate with Boas and Sapir, a position that partly comprehends and compromises the rational and universal, on the one hand, and the unique and historical, on the other; it does this through a theory of aesthetic form.

A series of erudite and adventurous thinkers and poets—most of them German—lived during or just after Kant's lifetime and developed in various ways the implications of his thought. Of these thinkers, Johann Gottfried von Herder (1774–1803), who was deeply indebted to Kant, propounded the view that poetic language is a psychological necessity, that poetry is an inevitable component of language, and that the organization of individual languages is unique. His voluminous writings and enthusiastic teaching greatly affected Johann Wolfgang von Goethe (1749–1832), whose clear perception of linguistic relativism is scattered throughout his writings ("He who doesn't know a foreign language, knows nothing of his own"). These and related ideas also spread to the leaders of English Romanticism such as Samuel Taylor Coleridge (1772–1832), who studied in Germany and communicated with Wordsworth, Shelley, and other shapers of what was a fundamentally new world view. Note, however, that these thinkers, while originators of romanticism, were also strongly classical in attitude and usually in training, so that linguistic relativism evolved in a context that transcended the conventional boundaries of these traditions. The synthetic Classical-Romantic position was exemplified perhaps most richly by Wilhelm von Humboldt (1767–1835), who elaborated the hypothesis of relativism and the central role in it of poetic language in its creative processual aspects; here we find yet another component of Sapir's philosophy. The general hypothesis continued to mature in the works of the great linguist and comparative psychologist Wilhelm Wundt (1832–1920) and others, mainly on the Continent.

Coming out of this tradition, Franz Boas (1858–1942) formulated yet another phase in the history of linguistic relativism that, following on Kant, stressed the categorical structure of knowing and perceiving. What was new was Boas's antievolutionary insistence on the intellectual equality of the world's natural languages—mainly as pertains to their phonologies and grammars. He substantiated this insistence with meticulous analyses of American Indian languages that, drawing on the attitudes of the natural sciences, brought an innovative refinement and sense of coherent program to our empirical methods of linguistic investigation. Many of his arguments about relativism were illustrated by long words or short sentences from American Indian languages that have a highly poetic quality, that are, as Sapir would put it, "like tiny imagist poems." The deeper levels of Boas's excitement about language were, I feel, aesthetic, just as his finest book in cultural anthropology was *Primitive Art.*

Boas's work was part of an international shift in the paradigms in terms of which language was understood. At about the same time, Benedetto Croce (1866–1952) was stating a philosophy in which language was the main vehicle and even the substance of intellectual and emotional values; following Vico, he gave a major role to poetry and claimed that language to a large extent was poetry. Approximately contemporaneous was Ernst Cassirer (1874–1945), who wrote voluminously on language and culture as symbolic systems and on the intimate relations between music, myth, and language (the latter often actually meaning *poetic* language). In Cassirer and, later, in Suzanne Langer (1895–) we see a tendency to resolve the conflict between reason and emotion, the universal and the unique, through a philosophy of aesthetic form. Again contemporaneous, and even more influential than Cassirer or Croce, was Ludwig Wittgenstein (1889–1951), who succeeded partly in demolishing the foundations of linguistic positivism and, in a fragmentary but penetrating way, explored some of the paradoxical interrelations between language, thought, and reality—the relativity of all thought to natural language. The fifth major figure of these times was the American Kenneth Burke (1897–), who like Wittgenstein mounted a strong attack on positivism. He stated clearly the importance of figurative and other poetic language in contrast to a positivistic semantics of objective reference. He also developed a comprehensive theory of literary form (e.g., tropes and genres), and pointed out many analogies between this and forms in culture and life generally; figures in art become analogues for figures in culture.

SARIR

The sixth major and roughly contemporary figure in this international contingent was Edward Sapir (1884–1939). Because of his importance in the context of anthropology and his focus on poetic language, a more detailed discussion of his contributions is called for.

Sapir had his origins in the sort of literary and philosophical tradition just sketched; a specialist in German philology, he wrote his master's thesis on Herder's philosophy of language and was steeped in historicism, Romanticism, and aesthetic studies of many kinds. Music, which he both studied and performed, was an important source of ideas throughout his life; in fact, there is such an extensive stratum of musical allusions in his writings that one could pull them together as a sort of proto-theory of the musical aspect of culture. Also decisive were the scientific ideas of his teacher Boas, American Indian linguistics, and the general linguistics of his day. Another obvious ingredient was the philosophy of Croce (and implicitly of Vico), which precipitated a sort of Copernican revolution in his thinking. It should be emphasized that Sapir was a wide-ranging, rapid-reading intellectual of his day; his position cannot be subsumed under any ism, and includes components from the social sciences, the humanities, and the arts. These components have many antecedents, just as Mozart eventually drew on Haydn, the Italians, the Bachs, and others to create a brilliant and completely personal synthesis. The way Sapir integrated diverse ideas and brought them to bear on the linguistic relativism hypothesis makes him its most legitimate eponym.

Several aspects of Sapir's position deserve elucidation here. First, the linguistic relativism hypothesis is contextualized in a relatively explicit idea of culture, seen as a historically derived, shared gestalt of patterns; language is always a part of culture, always the most formal and structured part, and usually the most important.

Second, the hypothesis is set in a comparativist's perspective of extraordinary scope; he was conversant with or analytically fluent in many languages from many parts of the world, and had a remarkable intuition for what appear to have been his native languages: English and, to a lesser extent, German and Yiddish. These intuitions are exemplified not only in his linguistics and poetry, but also by a natural, persuasive, and personal prose style. Analogously, we find a paradoxical synthesis of sensitivity to all manner of nuance and coloration in language with, on the other hand, a commitment to— and positive delight in—highly formal rigor, whether in music, mathematics, or linguistics. This seems, again analogously, to be concretized in the way he combines a formally precise practice of phonology with subtle intuitions for constructing sounds into poems (many of which seem to have been primarily explorations of sound structure—hence his otherwise perturbing excitement about poets such as Swinburne). Put yet another way, the (poetically) gross concepts of social science are integrated with relatively fine-grained concepts from poetry and poetics, the study of relativism here transcending the dichotomy between science and art.

Another paradox is the synthesis of a folk-psychological, basically Romantic tradition of "the genius of the people" with a keen theoretical taking-into-account of actual speakers and their interaction with their fellows (particularly, of course, poets and their audiences). An ultimate reality is always the experiencing, thinking, interacting, emotionally imaginative, speaking individual, and Sapir's concern with this individual imparts to many of his statements a peculiarly contemporary, phenomenological ring. Finally, we find a paradoxical synthesis of dense historicism and philology, on the one hand, with, on the other hand, an exact and penetrating view of synchronic structure.

This set of often paradoxical syntheses of combinations of typically discrete ideas, and Sapir's unique integration of anthropology, linguistics, and poetry/poetics, emerge in no one article or book on the linguistic relativism hypothesis, but in widely distributed sentences and paragraphs. His aptness, precision, and suggestiveness may not be unique, but surely they explain why he is quoted on relativism so often—often through passages that have been severed from the connections that he was trying to establish with poetry, the poet, and poetic language.

WHORF

The last major figure in the intellectual history that carries up to the 1940s was Benjamin Lee Whorf (1897–1941), who converted many components of what was a semi-oral scientific tradition into a fairly explicit and semipopularized philosophy. One of his particular contributions was to link the linguistic relativism hypothesis to gestalt psychology (just as Sapir linked it to depth and interactional psychology). He also linked it to the philosophy of the natural sciences, particularly physics, not only sketching or suggesting many parallels but coining the term "linguistic relativism." Moreover, he revived the early-nineteenth-century practice of connecting the linguistic relativism hypothesis with ideas deriving primarily from Oriental philosophy (e.g., the Upanishads). Finally, he added two specifically

American components: first, a generic pragmatism with brilliant examples of behavior (e.g., the gas drums that are so dangerous precisely because of the fumes not alluded to by their label "Empty"); second, a complex philosophical pragmatism that I associate with Peirce. I see in Whorf a continuation of the New England philosophy that originated as transcendentalism, particularly in his *vision* of language and his idea that language itself is a sort of vision—hence the often passionate acceptance of his works in this country. On the other hand, while he combined a superb comparativist perspective with a keen sense for the nuances of English, one misses in his formulations several critical ingredients in the linguistic relativism hypothesis, notably the unique individual as a semi-independent variable and poetry/poetics as providing some of the most critical data.

Whorf's exciting, monolithic claim is that basic ontology (or metaphysics or philosophy or world view—the terms are not sharply distinguished) is structured or determined or organized by language. Specifically, grammar is said to project the *form* for a cultural metaphysics. What the linguist-philosopher actually does is to work out the fragments of a notional grammar (e.g., categories of tense, gender, space, etc.) and then assert that its semantic meanings and associations are essentially the premises in a cultural world view; anecdotal evidence may be provided. The same claim for determinism is made at the practical or pragmatic level: "Agreement . . . is arrived at in human affairs . . . by linguistic processes, or else it is not reached" (Whorf 1964:212).

Such linguistic philosophy illustrates the linguist's position that equates language with thought or with culture, as Bloomfield, Benveniste, Chomsky, and many contemporaries have done. One obvious example, favored by Whorf and elucidated by Benveniste, is Aristotle's derivation of essences from the then-prevailing Greek grammar. But Whorf himself illustrates it by the way he and his stellar Hopi informant worked out a linguistic metaphysics. Similarly today, syntacticians work out the semantics of metaphor, anthropological linguists work out the rules of pragmatics, and both all too often equate their results with "culture" or "world view." In all such cases where grammar (or syntax or pragmatics) is the sole grist for the world view, we have world view indeed determined by grammar, through an obvious circularity. Whorf's extreme position on projecting a world view from grammatical axioms was significantly modified in his last article, published posthumously (1942), to the effect that "language is a superficial embroidery upon deeper processes of consciousness" (1964:239). But to see language as "superficial embroidery" is no more apt than the position regarding "axioms-cum-projections." The confusion between the two positions—neither of them tenable in pure form—also had the effect, during subsequent decades, of alienating many kinds of linguists, whose work I shall briefly summarize.

RECENT RESEARCH

The last three decades have witnessed many diverse contributions to the linguistic relativism hypothesis. One group of linguists sought "to test the Whorfian hypothesis" under quasi-laboratory conditions—for example, by measuring the speed with which speakers of different languages make rapid decisions on the color of objects, or by eliciting "native classifications" by asking the natives sets of pre-arranged questions. Leaving aside some grave methodological problems, the fact remains that most "ethnoscience," "componential analysis," and similar, self-consciously scientific approaches concluded—and in some sense demonstrated—that the effect of language on cognition, while small, was of a significant channeling or marginal order. By 1964, however, Burling could realistically write that the entire question of the linguistic relativism hypothesis had fallen "into disrepute" (1964:26); the hypothesis in conjunction with poetic language was generally ignored.

A second body of research during these decades did contribute to the linguistic relativism hypothesis, albeit implicitly in most cases. We find many meticulous analyses of universes of meaning, or, more concretely, of the semantic features underlying sets of words for colors, plants, and animals, for kinship and class (or caste), and for space, time, number, and the like—all of them implying that such drastically different language worlds must involve different levels of deep meaning, awareness, cognition, and consciousness generally. These explicit and suggestive cases became particularly strong when the language worlds in question were associated systematically with or contextualized in the perceptual process, patterns of ritual, life histories, or the daily, annual, or life cycle. Where the scholar's methods included mastering the language(s) in question and using them for fieldwork and for the exploration of poetic meanings in large bodies of texts, the insights into the linguistic relativism hypothesis were inevitable and considerable.

The linguistic relativism hypothesis is so complex that, while apparently being neglected, it may actually be under study and only waiting for a reformulation. Thus, dialectology and descriptive linguistics, despite a typically antiliterary thrust, have included some brilliant students of poetic variation. Transformationalism, while biased toward "nondeviant" language, abstract universals, and notational devices for basic reference, has also engendered important work on language and world view and on poetic language, notably on metrics and metaphor. Within anthropological linguistics a large (a) group of scholars—many of them students of Sapir or of his students (notably Hoijer)—have been analyzing the poetics of exotic, particularly American Indian, languages, translating poetries from around the world, and making contributions to a general theory of poetic semantics and performance. Within the structuralism of the Prague (b) School the issues raised by poetry and the profound insights it gives into language continued to be developed during these decades, often as a counter against extreme descriptivism or transformationalism. Indo-European and other philologically based linguistics, because of the highly poetic character of most of the texts, have yielded an enormous number of studies of specific tropes, genres, and styles. Psycholinguists, because of the analogical and poetic nature of so (c) much child language, have, despite a behaviorist bias, defined many new features in the ontogeny of poetic language that lend themselves in a suggestive way to the relation between language and world view in the culture of adults. Finally, sociolinguistics, while often (d) preoccupied with the statistical description of "objective data," has also yielded subtle analyses of the poetry of natural conversation, for example, and of indexical symbolism. In sum, a mass of recent research has contributed to our understanding of linguistic relativism and, to a lesser extent, poetic indeterminacy. There is so much evidence by now that we could probably speak of a theory; the burden of proof rests with those who claim that natural languages do *not* somehow constitute and engender fundamentally different points of view. While relativism may well have seemed to be in disrepute and poetry/poetics eclipsed, our knowledge of many component ideas and facts continued to grow in ways that, during the late 1970s, began to converge.

Let us turn now to one contemporary formulation of linguistic relativism, or linguistic-cultural relativism, and poetic indeterminacy.

3

Linguistic Relativism and Poetic Indeterminacy: A Reformulation of Sapir's Position

> Coyote said, "I am going to choke the Giant with this tamarack tree." The woman said, "You might as well throw that stick away. Don't you know you are already in the Giant's belly?"
>
> FLATHEAD MYTH *(Coffin, Indian Tales of North America)*

Let me start with something personal. I feel that American as against British English, and English of any major dialect as against Russian, and both languages as against the Tarascan language of Mexico constitute different worlds. I note that it is persons with experience of foreign languages and poetry who feel most acutely that a natural language is a different way not only of talking but of thinking and imaging and of emotional life. Rather than couch the issue in some qualified or weak form, let me follow my intuition of the realism and depth of one strong form of the hypothesis—one that, incidentally, rests on a vital tradition in philosophy and anthropological linguistics. This hypothesis falls into four interconnected assumptions, each with subdivisions.

First, I assume that the imagination of the unique individual, as carefully defined below, is a central reality, perhaps *the* central reality, of language and of its actualization in speech. In theoretical principle, of course, the imagination of the unique individual is only one of the major realities, along with linguistic structure, the here-and-now of dialogue, sociocultural context, and neurolinguistics and other material factors. However, given the persistent dominance today of "structure" in a sense that is not only societal but depersonalized, I wish, partly for heuristic reasons, partly as a matter of conviction, to emphasize the unique imagination. This factor of the unique imagination, in any case, works together with the ubiquity of context, the continuousness of meaning, and verbal beauty.

Second, language, whether at the individual, sociocultural, or some universal level, is inherently, pervasively, and powerfully poetic; this "poetic" is a matter of degree, with senses and levels that I will clarify. It is in poetry, properly speaking, that the poetic potential is most fully realized, through various kinds of intensification that call attention to the form of the message. This calling of attention must be consonant with the aesthetics, implicit and explicit, of the language and culture. Certain musical potentials of language, in particular, must work together with certain kinds of meaning, particularly mythic meaning: this is what below is called the poetic polarity.

Third, it is the relatively poetic nature of language, formed and articulated through figures of speech, that most deeply and massively affects the imagination—to the extent of seeming to be, paradoxically, not only its dress but its incarnation. The figures of language are constrained and structured by culture, whereas culture often moves, analogously, in the shape of figures.

Fourth and last, the partly indeterminate and hence partly free and even chaotic imagination interacts circularly, as a sort of feedback, with the poetic potential of language to create changes in meaning and sound.

Poetic language, in sum, is the locus of the most interesting differences between languages and should be the focus of the study of such differences. This hypothesis is unproven and unprovable, but so are the contrary hypotheses that derive everything from a universal mind or focus on the logical structure of propositions and the basic or atomic meanings of words. My hypothesis is also partly circular. Whether the twin flaws of partial circularity and unprovability deprive it of interest remains to be explored—and left to the judgment of the discriminating reader. Before entering into the main argument, let us consider what I take to be four prerequisites: the primary one of the imagination and the three ancillary ones of ubiquitous context, continuous meaning, and verbal beauty.

FOUR BASIC CONCEPTS

The Imagination

> The Brain—is wider than the Sky—
> For—put them side by side—
> The one the other will contain
> With ease—and You—beside—
> EMILY DICKINSON *(no. 632)*

The idea most fundamental to my thesis is that of the imagination. By "the imagination" I mean the processes by which individuals integrate knowledge, perceptions, and emotions in some creative way which draws on their energies in order that they may enter into new mental states or new relations with their milieu. My idea clearly emphasizes the emotions, imagery and image use, sensuous imagery above all (dreams), aesthetic apprehension, and the more mythic side of life. But one also speaks of the scientific imagination or of the imaginative farmer, and by the same token the imagination includes cognition, literal description, and reason—concrete, abstract, and practical. The imagination in these senses analyzes and even breaks down meanings. It also synthesizes, freely constructing idea systems and perceptual images and myths; the imagination quintessentially mediates between analysis and synthesis. But it is also passive in receiving, absorbing, and responding to information and feelings, and in this passivity, too, it functions creatively in linguistic and other symbolic processes. The imagination—this yin and yang of the mind, with its gamut of mental life and its freedom—resembles Whitehead's idea of apprehension. On the other hand, it differs greatly from "mind" and "thought" in their usual rational meanings, which, wittingly or unwittingly, have prejudged most approaches to linguistic relativity. The creative and significantly chaotic imagination emerges with the sense of the self and its integrity that is partly instilled and partly created by individuals, during maturation within their culture and society. The imagination, in all its individuality, is also where freedom in language enjoys maximum scope and outlet.

There is no meaning without the partly chaotic, imaginative individual. Even the supposedly inherent or irreducible denotations abstracted and operated on by the logician entail individual values and an academic context and hence imply considerable indeterminacy. The imagination is always in flux in time and space within shifting contexts.

Contexts

The shifting contexts are of many kinds. The first is primarily verbal, be it the written text or some place in the stream of spoken discourse or, on the other hand, the underlying sound system and other parts of the grammar being used.

The basic phrase "I saw," when translated into Homeric Greek, would necessarily imply a force going out from the eyes and acting on the object seen. When translated into Tarascan it would have to imply something about the degree of certitude in the seeing ("definitely saw," "was reported as seen," and so forth). Even in English it is fundamentally ambiguous.

Or to take a second example, proper names, contrary to what most logicians say, have many meanings, sometimes in dense adumbration. Along a scale of masculinity we can range names such as Mark and Joe, then Ray and Paul, then names that are sometimes bestowed on women, such as Lynn, and finally names with feminine or even effeminate connotations. But the dimension of masculinity is only one of many in the semantics of names. All such meanings are sensitive to contexts that, taken together, constitute a galaxy of contexts.

Context is often a matter of situation: a specific reading by a poet, a specific inning in a baseball game. Or it may involve classes of such situations: poetry readings, baseball games. As Whorf put it, even "scientific terms are, without exception, sensitive to context: 'electrical' in 'electrical apparatus' is not the same as 'electrical expert' . . . referents of scientific terms are often conveniently vague . . . scientific terms like 'force, average, sex, allergic, biological' are not less pitiful and, in their own way, no more certain in reference than 'sweet, gorgeous, rapture, enchantment, heart and soul, star dust. . . . You have probably heard of 'star dust'—what is it? Is it a multitude of stars, a sparkling powder, the soil of the planet Mars, the Milky Way, a state of daydreaming, a poetic fancy, pyrophoric iron, a spiral nebula, a suburb of Pittsburgh, or a popular song?" (1964:260–61).

Context implies that all meaning is a matter of degree, probability, multiplicity, and, from the individual's point of view, indeterminacy. The word "cuticle" practically always refers to a body part, and such relatively simple symbols, or symbols with simplified meanings, work as tokens in a great deal of conversation. Their shifting but minimal meanings do need to be shared by natives in order for them to agree and, to a lesser extent, disagree with each other. Most natives in all cultures assume some such minima. In this sense there is "basic meaning." But even these basic cases decide nothing absolutely, because "cuticle" means differently to different speakers and to some can even mean a non–body part; there are languages such as Russian that lack a special word for the hardened skin at the back and sides of a fingernail.

At the other extreme of multiplicity and indeterminacy, a word such as "code" lacks one primary meaning, and the mathematical shape of its underlying meanings—to the extent that there is one— can vary from a cube to a chain, and so forth; one linguist, Martin Joos, found that each of the ten main meanings overlapped with two others so that the entire set could be mapped as a circle.

The great majority of symbols are clearly ambiguous, albeit less so than "code." The words "mother" and "red" often involve kinship and color but can mean a multitude of things in a multitude of contexts—as we find when we hear them put together in "red mother." "Mother" can imply "the woman who bore and/or raised me up." But it also implies its counterpart, child, and its adjunct, father, and prior existence. It may imply nurturance of the mothered child or conflict with the father, depending on the culture. By "culture" I mean such things as world view and, more precisely, the meanings and patterns shared and transmitted by one or more individuals— meanings that may be sensuous and practical as well as abstract and ideological. The farther we move in terms of culture, situation, and individual, the more meanings a symbol turns out to have; there is no limit. Let us leave the idea of meaning without social context to the logician's paradise "where it is easy to be right": there remains the more useful idea of implication or association—the potential meanings of a symbol in relation to other symbols and in all culturally relevant contexts.

The questions become more acute as we move to more complex words and into longer statements of increasing ambiguity. Is Yeats's "Isle of Innisfree" about roughing it on an island, or about urban nostalgia, or about his response to Thoreau's *Walden*? The ambiguity of poems, as of conversations, has long been understood. Wordsworth put it sarcastically: "A primrose by the river's brim / A yellow primrose was to him / And it was nothing more." The primary fact of linguistic experience is a differential but continuous ambiguity of meaning.

Basic versus Continuous Meaning

Contrasting with such continuous ambiguity is the notion that semantic space is filled with words or similar symbols that basically, really mean one thing. This notion, deriving as much from popular usage as from any genuine theory, carries with it several misguided notions. These include the so-called objectivity of observable phenomena, together with the existence of clear boundaries around words and ideas, as though they were objects (and as though such objects and our perceptions of them had sharp boundaries). Another, larger boundary is assumed to demarcate all such objectlike, cognitive ideas from other kinds of experience. Finally, these object-ideas exist with considerable uniformity, fixed in a static space.

The linguists and other students of language who adhere to this notion of atomic, cognitive meanings and mechanistic structures often see their job as identifying sets of signs and contexts and then matching them with each other in terms of projections, derivations, transformations, and other quasi-mathematical operations. The fixed idea of atomic, cognitive meanings, pervasive in so many fields of study, goes under diverse names, including denotation, innate universals, irreducible meaning, essential meaning, reference, basic meaning, and so forth. My own purpose in expounding the relativity-indeterminacy hypothesis is similar to Whitehead's in his critique of materialism in physics, when, as he put it, he tried "to edge cognitive reality away from being the necessary substratum of experience" (1948:93). The idea that such a cognitive substratum is basic is fundamentally alien to linguistic relativism and poetic indeterminacy.

Verbal Beauty

As we edge this cognitive stratum away we find ourselves, particularly in poetry, entering a different universe which has been intuited from time immemorial. Horace and Wallace Stevens both insisted that here language must amuse; Housman stipulated that "the pit of his stomach receive something like a spear" (Ellmann and O'Clair 1973:97); the poetry magazine editor may scribble on your margin, "It's got to grab my guts (poetically)." Whole philosophies about this universe rest on ideas of play, wish fulfillment, emotion, technique and form, isolation and equilibrium, empathy and truth, tension and release; there are yet others. This multiplicity, however, should not obscure the fact that these philosophers agree on the existence of what they are trying to explain.

My own feeling is that poetic beauty is a tenuous mediation between two things. First, the usual levels and compartments of language are partly altered, even merged and broken, in ways that suggest the novel, the primordial, or the chaotic. Simultaneously, we find that the language conforms in some degree to the levels, boundaries, and rules of a poetic tradition or some analogous, special style. This dynamic verbal counterpoint between uncertainty and harmony largely creates the sense of beauty. At a vaguer but equally meaningful level, poetic beauty arises from a mediation between different intuitions of reality and irreality and, on the other hand, the more elusive sonic vibrations of a language.

Values of poetic beauty figure in all cultures, and every language has expressions for them, with many distinctions, gradations, and overlappings in meaning (as in Western aesthetics) between "elegant," "fine-sounding," "musical," and the like. The exact form and content of the beautiful in a given culture can be and sometimes have been established in a rigorous and empirical, experimentally based manner. But even if they hadn't been, the perils of labeling and definition do not justify omitting the ideal of beauty from our model or ignoring the more organized forms that it may take, whether public or private. Among other things, the cultural aesthetics and the individual's intention to realize them add another, valid criterion for distinguishing, however approximately, between advertisements and poems. The ideal of beauty, again, is relative and contextual: some excellent poems are in certain real senses ugly, whereas some verbal phenomena—like Daisy's voice in *The Great Gatsby*—may be of matchless verbal beauty but not be part of a poem.

Some value of beauty is a fact of life for poetry, but also for baseball and plowing and the so-called art of war. This wide scope of beauty may reassure the reader for whom the mere phrase "poetic language" triggers mental static or an onrush of irrelevant associations. Here I think especially of the scientistic social scientist, who, unlike the Tarascan or the theoretical physicist, sees a chasm between art and science, truth and beauty, and fears it.

"Poetic language" is the best name for the following discussion of "technical" dimensions such as figurative language and the poetic polarity.

FIGURES OF LANGUAGE

The Poetic Structure of Language (e.g., Conversation)

The second part of my hypothesis of linguistic relativity holds that all natural language is poetic in part. Our concern with this poetry is heightened by a keen awareness of the humdrum, practical, relatively topical and referential nature of the great mass of actually occurring speech forms of most conversations in our society. Almost all conversation is, at the surface, literally formulaic in the sense of conjoining and interlocking prefabricated words, phrases, and other units (Leech 1969: 26–27). This is particularly so in the case of hurried people with practical jobs to get done: the personnel in an understaffed intensive care ward. One intermediate stage beyond these situations is advertising and political rhetoric, where the insidious possibilities of language are exploited by the coiners and persuaders. Another intermediate step beyond these situations is where conversational prefabs are juxtaposed and contextualized in relatively imaginative ways; many a published poem is built of conversational prefabs just as much oral-epic poetry is built from poetic prefabs and formulae. In terms of deeper levels, below behavior, in any case, poetry is a ubiquitous potential in any language and it may surface often in the case of some individuals and/or contexts, be it constructing a simile from prefabs, or juxtaposing two well-worn words to make a fresh metonym (or hearing the metonym in a haphazard juxtaposition).

The pervasiveness of poetry has been argued again and again. "Poetry is nothing extraordinary; it is only the words which rise from the heart and lie at the tip of the tongue," as a Chinese scholar put it (see Liu 1974: 73). Or as Robert Frost says: "All thinking, except mathematical thinking, is metaphorical" (1966: 36–37). Or the contemporary philosopher, Nelson Goodman (1976: 80): "Metaphor permeates all discourse, ordinary and special, and we should have a hard time finding a purely literal paragraph anywhere. In the last prosaic enough sentence, I count five sure or possible—even if tired—metaphors." This is also part of what the physicist Heisenberg had in mind when he wrote (1958: 168): "Words are not so clearly defined as they seem to be at first sight . . . the intriguing uncertainty of words was of course recognized very early." With these words of wisdom in mind, let us now include our scientistic social scientist under the scope of the Spanish proverb: "Of musician, poet, and idiot, we all have got a little bit." Because through the ages and disciplines and across the lands the reality is not poetry versus nonpoetry but more poetry versus <u>less</u> poetry. Poetic language permeates ordinary language, and also technical languages.

What do I mean by the heavily laden term "poetic language"? Most obviously, I mean all parts of a language system that exemplify a figure; for instance, metaphorlike relations in grammar are latent in the long words of Tarascan (see below) just as they are in English idioms ("That idea is off the wall"). Just as obvious would be the first-time creations of anyone being poetic in some conventional sense: minting a riddle or a stanza or *hearing* the fineness in a snatch of conversation. Somewhat less clear is the enormous interstitial area of both structure and actual speech that may evince analogical freshness or ambiguity: "She wet her lips" can mean many things. At the other extreme is the smaller core of words, idioms, and constructions with relatively fixed and frozen meanings—something like "the car stopped," or "a little girl." That even such simple tokens are pregnant with poetry jumps to reverberating life as soon as we juxtapose and, inevitably, fail to translate "a little girl" into "ein kleines Mädchen," or "une petite fille," or "una muchachita." The relativity of translation at this simple level suggests the heteromorphism of all languages and the mathematical power of the poetic potential in all natural languages.

Poetic language is actualized in all domains of life, even the logician's study, and is common in cafeterias, bars, streets, at kitchen tables and conveyor belts—wherever one argues, persuades, seduces, reports, creates rapport, or otherwise communicates—and particularly in moments of playfulness, humor, trauma, crisis, and strong emotion. Some of this, notably play and persuasion, abounds in the banal poetry of advertising: "So round, so firm, so fully packed, so free and easy on the draw" does not, in contexts such as the Johnny Carson show, immediately suggest a cigarette.

This everyday, quotidian poetry is easily illustrated from within the domain of baseball by epithets running from "Catfish" Hunter to "The Yankee Clipper." The World Series stimulates a torrent of figures: "The Dodger infield can make a routine grounder into a trip up the Amazon" (1981). And all sports have semifrozen metaphors that probably survive because of their aptness: in football, a runner "finds a seam," a quarterback "threads the needle," and a tackler "rings his bell" (referring to the helmet and the brains of the runner).

In the excerpt from a long poem cited below, I tried to garner some of this poetry in ordinary language by taking about seventy of the more pithy and essential lines from a very original book about Joe DiMaggio by Maury Allen (*Where Have You Gone, Joe DiMaggio?*), which was based on interviews with over 250 persons. These line-long sentences were then arranged into stanzas in terms of what seemed to be the inner dynamics of that part of the story of "Joe D." Here is one of those stanzas:

"The thing about DiMaggio is he always gave a thousand percent
    every game."
"I was cocky, confident . . . but I kept it inside myself, inside
    the shell."
"Joe is probably the most self-effacing guy I have ever met."
"A very lonely man at times." "An introvert in those days."
    "Tense."
Thirty half-cups of coffee a day, one or two packs of Camels.
"He never seemed to be able to let loose and just enjoy himself."
"Joe wasn't a guy you could kid around with in the training room."
"He had a toughness and coldness with strangers, sort of guards
    himself,
But all that seems to break down with the kids. They adore him."
DiMag: "There might be a kid in the stands, or five or ten
who never had seen me play or would never see me play again.
I burned in the belly to be the best there was for them,
to leave them with a good impression of me."

Another example comes from the Afro-American youth of the ghettos, as reported by Labov: "Your mother so skinny she ice-skate on a razor blade . . . so low she can play Chinese handball on a curb . . . so low, got to look down to look up . . . so black she sweat chocolate. . . . (1972: 279)" These and similar expressions are said to figure in the style called "rapping," the purpose of which, according to Brown, is to bring the participant to tears or to attacking his mocker. "Rapping" and "styling" are, of course, part of a much larger inventory of Black English conversational styles.

We also have the massive evidence collected from Russian preschoolers and presented by Chukovsky. For example: "Can't you see? I'm barefoot all over." "Daddy, look how your pants are sulking." "A turkey is a duck with a bow around its neck." "The sea has one shore but a river has two." "Please don't cut down this pine tree—it makes the wind." "Now I know where the night hides itself." "I know how the stars are made. They make them from what is left over from the moon." "I'm a why-er, you are a becauser." "Who gave birth to the first mother?" "The rooster, could he completely, completely forget that he is a rooster, and lay an egg?" "Out of what does one make people? out of bones?" Even this small set includes several kinds of metaphor. And there are various metonyms: the anatomical ("I'm barefoot all over"), the taxonomic ("a turkey is a duck"), and so forth. In fact, the hundreds of examples in the book would fill all the slots in a highly elaborated scheme of tropes. The apparent exceptions, such as pervasive syntactic parallelism, would reflect, not the absence of such patterns from among Russian preschoolers, but the nature of the samples used for this semipopular work about their speech.

Poetry is in the speech around us, often when not expected. Many persons not recognized as poets can, nevertheless, match the poet in verbal wizardry, despite the latter's exceptional aptitudes and motivation. And while rigorous formal schooling has been a prerequisite for success in some poetic traditions, as in medieval Ireland, imperial China, and, increasingly, the United States today, the unbudgeable fact is that many of the world's poetic masterpieces have been wrought by poets with little or no formal training—or indeed, little if any higher literary education (in English, for example, Chaucer, Shakespeare, Blake, Burns, Keats, Poe, Whitman, Melville, Dickinson, Hardy, Lawrence, Frost, and yet others, come to mind—and English may be exceptional in this regard as compared to the other major traditions in European languages). The poet, then, alchemizes through a special process from the prodigious skills that are mastered by every native speaker and used by everyone every day. Poetry thus differs from most other formal contemporary arts, with their indispensable, specialized, and intellectually complex training.

The native speaker matrix of poetic language and poetry underlies the linguist Kiparsky's contention that in poetry, in contrast to painting and music, "no truly new forms have emerged." In poetry, we still live in a universe of parallelism, metaphor, and essentially archaic sound textures, a universe conditioned by the meanings of ordinary language in conversations, newspaper clippings, and so forth. A related point is argued by the poet Gary Snyder, who regards "the streams of civilized tradition [as] having their roots in the paleolithic . . . the Shaman-poet is simply the man whose mind reaches easily into all manner of shapes and other lives, and gives song to dreams. Poets have carried this function forward through all civilized times" (1973:395–99). Poetry, in other words, in its paleolithic nature and cross-linguistic complexity is analogous to grammar, where, "when it comes to linguistic form, Plato walks with the Macedonian swineherd, Confucius with the head-hunting savage of

Assam" (Sapir 1921a : 234). I am convinced that the poet-linguist who wrote these lines was thinking of poetic language as one quintessence of linguistic form, since Confucius and Plato were poets as well as philosophers (the quote, incidentally, constitutes a neat one-sentence poem). The relation between poetry and conversation is a continuum, as Tannen has argued, in two clear senses: they constantly interact with each other, and the difference between them is one of degree. Yet we find enormous variation in individual and cultural attitudes toward the relations between the language of poems and the language of conversation—and other, less obviously poetic discourse.

Let us look at some of this variation. Many poems in the current work of young Americans are indistinguishable from snippets of fairly humdrum conversation. For example, a recent book marketed as poetry consists of paragraph-long quotations from a series of ball players (with facing portrait) that are rarely more poetic than any other set of paragraphs that might have been selected at random. (The lines from Joe DiMaggio cited above are more poetic). At the other extreme from this "uncovered art," Musil (1928 : 284) tells us that among the Bedouins "the words used in a poem must be out of the ordinary, not those heard in everyday life. The more unusual the words the Bedouin can put into his composition, the better he thinks it is." But even in the Bedouin's Arabic or the highly conventional art languages of early Greece and T'ang China we may assume a creative underlying dialogue between the poet's poetic language and the lilt and inflections and rhythm of his or her conversation. The same holds today for such intensely literary and literarily decadent poets in English as Ashbery. In the case of a genius such as Sappho or Frost the poem may seem quite conversational but also be poetic in some rigorously conventional and formal sense.

The relation between poetic and natural language is not cyclical but rather that of two imperfectly parallel streams, which sometimes are almost out of earshot of each other and sometimes converge. A poet with a new vision of verbal music may approximate and partially identify with actual speech, as did Donne and Frost. This drawing near may be followed by decades during which the lesser or more formal potentials of the original vision are elaborated by epigones and acolytes, some of whom may be unaware of whom they are imitating. And these approximations to living speech are always shadowed by the artifice that is indispensable to poetry. Beneath the conversational formulae in New Hampshire dialect the knowledgeable reader can also hear the strict meter and the artifice of Frost's favorite poet, Horace:

> They gave him back to her. The letter came
> Saying . . . And she could have him. And before . . .
> (Frost, "Not to Keep")

Whether poetic language is nearly identical to conversation or vastly different, it should not be thought of as deviant or deformed, as has been claimed by some, but rather as a distinct style with its own grammar and patterns of usage. Again, while some individuals are creative with language, much usage is poetic without being particularly individual: the exchange of formulaic obscenities, for example, or the interlarding of unintelligible Sanskrit phrases in modern Indian folk texts. Sapir put these matters of degree with typical urbanity:

> Have we been talking verse all our lives without knowing it? . . . Verse, to put the whole matter in a nutshell, is *rhythmically self-conscious* speech or discourse. . . . Opening [the book that lies nearest to hand] at random, the first sentence that strikes my eye is: "uniforms and badges promote brotherhood." I am convinced that this is meant to be prose. Nevertheless, when I read it many times . . . I gradually find myself lulled in the lap of verse . . . Had [the author] chosen to clothe his rhythmic pattern in words of poetic connotation, say: "Thunderbolts come crashing in mad turbulence," the effect of verse latent in all prose would have risen to the surface far more rapidly (1921b:223)

Some Specific Figures

Language is figured, so let us consider some of its individual figures, of different scopes and at different levels. One common figure depends on the relation of part to whole, as in the fingers of Homer's rosy-fingered dawn. The constructional figure of syntactic parallelism characterizes early Hebrew, Walt Whitman, and many individual rhetorical and personal styles. Irony, to take another, combines mockery, sarcasm, and deceptiveness with the assumption of two or more audiences; the Socratic variant implies an audience that is "in the know" as against a second party that is being led by Socrates' wit (which wit, incidentally, depends on Greek attitudes toward artful mendacity). Another poetic figure is the outcry; in *King Lear*, the blinding scene with its "Out, vile jelly!" has an expressiveness from the brutalized blinder's point of view that was as in tune with the culture of Elizabeth's time as it would have been discordant to that of Queen Victoria. Or again, the figure of the proverb, so natural to proverb-oriented cultures such as peasant Spain and Russia—as well as long chains of proverbs with an interproverb structure—emerges as an irresistible component in the philosophically central positions of Sancho Panza and, in *War and Peace*, of the peasant Platon Karataev. The figure of the enigma, the mystifying riddle, or the deliberately obscured gist, all with their threat to reason, serves to organize and motivate not only the skaldic poetry of Old Iceland, but much Modernist poetry as well and the poems (and repartee, debate, and other discourse) in many other specific traditions. To sum up: part-whole, parallelism, irony, outcry, proverb, and enigma suggest the incredible richness and sheer quantity of figures that writhe within language, waiting to be exploited or working on their own.

Other figures are less obvious and less conventionally recognized. Even relations of cause and effect, although basically logical, can work as figures in poetry where narrative and argument are decisive; one example would be the closing lines in many sonnets that resolve a stylized paradox. Indeed, mathematical operations may serve: witness the geometrical figures in Donne or Dickinson or the intermittent and usually latent set theory in some poetry today.

Most of these figures of speech or, more technically, "tropes," are partly independent of each other, and generally no one is reducible to any other, although all can be comprised in master schemes or taxonomies of tropes; my own has six major categories: imagistic, modal, analogical, contiguity tropes, formal-constructional, and expansion-condensation. Within any such scheme a given trope will have to be cross-classified because each trope, while partly independent, also partly interdepends with other tropes, so that an instance of one will entail others. This is one thing that makes poetic language so complicated, since even a single word in context involves a plurality of tropes. Among the major tropes, the counterpointing of sound texture with nuances of mythic meaning is surely the most essential, the "macro-trope" (as will be further argued below). The tropes of poetic language in their overall schemata, frequencies, and internal structure vary, of course, from one culture to another, and from one poet, poetician, or ordinary native to another.

The Limited Metaphor

Many persons still feel that the master figure of them all is based on a pleasing, or at least striking and nonobvious, similarity—between, for instance, an ash leaf and a painted eyebrow. But, as Goodman has argued, such similarities work (that is, are beautiful) only when they combine "novelty with fitness . . . the odd with the obvious"; when, that is, relative to the language and the individual, the similarity is neither too close and comprehensive nor too distant and obscure in meaning. Metaphor may also bridge, not two simple symbols, but two or more complex processes—up to a point.

"Metaphor," once a precise term, has grown loose in popular and technical usage. For example, a poem that leads us through an inferno has been called a metaphor for pathological obsessions—by a critic, not by the poet, Dante, who was also a theorist of poetry. Similarly, natural language has been called "a metaphor of the world," or, to switch quotes, "the world is a metaphor of language"; but in each of these cases the poets were self-consciously using the word "metaphor" metaphorically. Little has been won, on the other hand, by those poeticians who extend the metaphor until it becomes a catch-all for allegory, conceit, or anything involving similarity. The wolf hunt in *War and Peace* ended with the downing, gagging, and mocking of a she-wolf to the extent that the entire episode becomes a complex, sustained, and many-pointed analogy to a gang rape and, in the epic itself, to the subsequent seduction of the main heroine by a collusion of high-society characters—these are macro-metaphors, if you will, but not metaphors. The *omnium gatherum* use of metaphor reflects Aristotle, more recent theory, and some ethnic, historical, and personal biases. Even in its narrow meaning the role of metaphor varies enormously between poems, poets, poetic traditions, and cultures; the salience of metaphor as a trope is low, for example, in some American Indian traditions. There are other good reasons, including the need for theoretical clarity, for keeping metaphor down at a level where it contrasts with such other tropes as irony, parallelism, the abstraction of gist, the riddle, and, also, the part-whole figure, or metonym.

It is the more powerful and comprehensive processes of analogy and, psychologically speaking, association that include metaphor and many other tropes and that typify myth and, even more, poetry; witness the mind-boggling shifts of Pindar from one mythic image to another via shared, transitional, perceptual images. Despite the way analogy governs poetry, however, there is no sharp boundary between analogical and other modes of thought (any more than these are clearly compartmentalized in the brain). Almost all poems are logical and discursive to a degree, just as all scientific discourse is significantly analogical; and the purest logic may be transmuted into tropes, as in *Alice in Wonderland.*

Figures and Culture

What is a trope to the critic may be a trick for the poet, and in either case there are fascinating cultural constraints. One piquant example involves the pepper plant (the semantics of which, incidentally, has become an academic classic because of a Philippine language reported to have a deep taxonomy with a terminal node known as the "cat's penis"). In the Cuna language of Panama, we find a native taxonomy with fifty-three terminal nodes referring to kinds of hot pepper. In a curing chant called "The Way of the Hot Pepper," these terminal nodes are arranged into a parallelistic verse pattern; that is, the sets in the taxonomy are projected onto the horizontal life of the chant (Sherzer 1983:32–33). Concludes Cuna specialist Sherzer (personal communication): "The taxonomy of pepper includes both elements that actually occur in nature and spiritual types of pepper relevant to the curing processes . . . a semantic pattern which is not one-to-one with nature. It is part of the Cuna world view as seen through language. But not by everyone and not at all times and places. Rather, in the poetic magic or magical poetry of the text specialist and his audience." The poetry of peppers shows us once again that every natural "fact" is an emblem of a mental fact, as Emerson argued so eloquently.

The Cuna way of projecting folk taxonomies and inventories onto the horizontal line of verse typifies much poetry and song, ballads and chants, and children's verse. It also typifies some high traditions, whether embodied in Hesiod's *Theogony* or in many passages that come to mind from Herrick and other sixteenth- and seventeenth-century poets, as well as from Walt Whitman. More recently, Snyder wrote, in "Hunting 13," "Now I'll tell you what food we lived on: Mescal, yucca fruit. . . ." and so on through forty-seven other nature foods (not including peppers). Such projection from the vertical axis of items selected to the horizontal one of the line or utterance is of course general for language, except that in poetry it is intensified by special conventions and goals, including those of marking: for example, the selection from a reservoir of words ending in -*ump* and, within that, of better as against worse rhymes. On the other hand, the projection of taxonomies in Cuna illustrates the many differences of form and frequency between poetry and conversation; in conversation, lists are common, whereas a taxonomy, while rare in conversation, is often built into primitive poetry and may serve as a mnemonic device.

Culture, obviously, may constrain those levels of language that symbolize natural objects. American English, for example, does not compel us to see the serrate edge of a leaf in an eyebrow, but this comparison was customary, almost obligatory, in the semiformulaic art language of T'ang China, where courtesans even painted their eyebrows green. At the other extreme, an abstract or relational category such as a part of speech may anchor a speech rule or a cultural ritual. In Navajo, Reichard (1963:294) reports, "the verbs of action and motion are differentiated by a rather simple tense system— present, past and future—and a complicated aspect system—progressive, momentary, customary, inceptive, and cessative. Often, therefore, the burden of a song has a tense or aspect change to indicate the progression from a wish to an accompaniment." Other kinds of language-intensive symbolism are somewhere between the concrete and the relational, or articulated with both levels.

In addition to obliging or being suggestive, language also may block poetic imaging and associations; Sappho's line about "sleep dropping down through leaves that quiver" cannot be translated into Tarascan (nor, probably, Navajo), where sleep and the like do not drop. Similarly, the multifarious English idioms in "thing" ("to know everything"), which imply an object-oriented world view, usually translate into Russian verbs without overt objectives or with non-thing objects. Whole classes of constructions, genres, and tropes may be blocked by such explicit or implicit conventions: the proverb, while, rare in some native American literatures, as noted, is a master trope in some African ones.

Obligatory versus nonobligatory should not come to constitute a hard-cutting dichotomy. The phrase, "the most unkindest cut of all," which Shakespeare puts in the mouth of Marc Antony as the latter is describing the assassination of Julius Caesar, does not illustrate so-called poetic licence, as is claimed; nonpoets are often just as licentious. What it does illustrate is the sense of this poet for one way that emotional breakdown can be mirrored in speech and exploited in rhetoric (the line, incidentally, scans regularly). Most if not all obligatory rules are broken or modified in certain contexts, just as context affects the inevitable variation of nonobligatory rules.

These rules often run deep in the linguistic unconscious of all but the more sophisticated and self-conscious linguist-poetician. Walt Whitman's long lines often are anchored, as is claimed (Fussell

1978 : 305), by a phrase or word such as "arrangement" that consists of an unstressed, a stressed, and an unstressed syllable. But was the poet—to say nothing of his reader—aware of this probabilistic rule of the final amphibrachic foot, and how often did this awareness affect his writing? In other cases the rules are well known and even discussed heatedly by many people, as seems to have been true of the sonnet in Renaissance Italy. Yet other rules, norms, patterns, and so forth hold for the culture in general, and are only incidentally made grist for poems. In any case, the thousands of poetic and potentially poetic rules and tricks and habits are handled (used or responded to) by the native in a natural manner—just as he speaks without a foreign accent and notices one in another speaker. It is these poetic levels that the linguist, particularly the non-native one, rarely tries to ascertain, rarely mentions in the grammar, and neglects in the dictionary. And yet it was the theoretically adamant descriptive linguist, Bloomfield, who epitomized the vast relation when he wrote, "Poetry is the blazoned book of language" (1933 : 443), to which, since it is true, one might add, "And language implies, among other things, *rough drafts* for poetry." In different words, language can be seen as an infinitude of used poems waiting to be molded into new realities as one determines, and fails to determine, the degree and direction to which one will be influenced by them.

Figures and Reflexivity

If we grant that "verse is latent in all prose," just how does the poet make it surface by means of intensification? In part by word choice, phrasing, and so forth that call attention to their own form, as in Dylan Thomas's "Fern Hill":

> Now as I was young and easy under the apple boughs
> About the lilting house and happy as the grass was green.

Such beckoning by the poem always implies a comment of some sort on the underlying linguistic code—where grass alliterates with green, but houses do not lilt. Culturally specialized variants of poetic language that so beckon to themselves are, for example, the oral traditions, where most parts of most lines are built from prefabricated formulae that are known or at least felt as such—where, for instance, "barren" and "wine-dark" exhaust what you can attribute to the sea with an adjective. But while such formulaic building blocks hypertypify Homer and Serbian epic, they actually are integral to almost all poets and poetic languages, from Sappho to Ashbery. Going further, the great bulk of ordinary conversation is literally formulaic in the way it conjoins and interlocks rote-known words, phrases, and other units. Some of these conversational prefabs, like "Pass the salt," are as close to being purely referential as one can get in language, but the great majority of pat phrases and idioms—for example, "catch the bus"—transparently conceal figures of speech; in fact, that is one source of their vitality and usefulness.

Often the poet intensifies language by challenging or even to some extent remaking the underlying code or codes, as in the multiple syntactic styles of Cummings. Or he may interrelate several dialects, or comment on speech—for example, Tolstoy on the grammaticality or code-switching of his protagonists. At a banal but still poetic level, Dizzy Dean used to quip, "Lots of folks that don't say ain't, ain't eatin'." In these and other ways language may remind the speaker of itself. The controversy as to whether language reflects back on the poem itself, or on the making of the poem, or on the poetic language in general, or on sound and words actually in the line is spurious: any of these processes is reflexive and each implies the others. The multiple reflexivity of all poetic language is partly shaped by the individual's imagination, but, because language is a feedback process, the on-going, imaginative creation is also organized by the on-going flow of the poem or of other discourse.

The way poetic language reflects back on itself (or "creates a set toward the message") entails the use of forms that are more or less marked. Such marking may be at any level, from a subtly phonetic one to the more obvious techniques of alliteration and rhyme. Marking may involve extraordinary morphological selections—take Hopkins's wild last line from "The Wreck of the Deutschland," with three possessives in each hemistich: "Our hearts' charity's hearth's fire, our thoughts' chivalry's throng's Lord." At the level of vocabulary the word "flame" might replace an expected "fire," or "fire" might be used in an unanticipated context: "the all-consuming fire of his inaninity." Aesthetic effects are achieved, whether through the choice of marked forms or through the use of unmarked forms in contexts that mark them. Syntactic marking is at least as frequent as any other kind, as in Dickinson's highly marked, "Yet know I how" as against the less marked "Yet I know how" or the unmarked "But I know how" (these options, as always, fall into a sliding scale). Markings with form and context are one way to create a subtler and deeper language, and they may delight the poet to the extent of becoming self-conscious devices. But whether the marking be artful or totally ingenuous, the result must slant, tilt, and glitter, as in Shakespeare's Sonnet 65:

> How with this rage shall beauty hold a plea,
> Whose action is no stronger than a flower?

Even those poets and conversationalists who try to eschew style on the ground that "it destroys what it illuminates," manage to achieve a sort of intensity willy-nilly because their consistent avoidance of known options within the context of familiar ones generates a stylized antistyle in its own right. Out of such diverse markings, in any case, poets and people speaking poetically give new life to their languages.

THE MASTER TROPE

> And all my soul is in the bells,
> But music will not save me from the abyss.
> OSIP MANDELSTAM, *"The Pedestrian"*

The Poetic Polarity: Music

Language, as argued above, is an infinitude of used or potential poems waiting to be molded into new realities by the individual. Language is rough drafts for poetry, just as poetry is "the blazoned book of language."

This "blazoned book" gets written by drawing on two sources. One is the sounds of human language in general and of the poet's language in particular, that is, the vast network of associations that ranges from subtle phonetic nuance to features that discriminate basic meanings ("sack" versus "shack"), matters of order and hierarchy, many levels of intonation, and, of course, the interweaving of all this with the grammatical, semantic, and sociocultural universe (the *sh* of "shibboleth"). This sound system is partly controlled by principles of musical composition.

Poets have written suggestively about this linguistic music. Williams and others deal with the poetic function of the syllable, the line, the breath group, the tone level of vowels. Frost speaks of the thousands of little sets of what he calls "sentence sounds," each with an overall feel—for example, "Well, I swan!"—and of the energy that comes from synthesizing such sounds of whole utterances with the traditional forms of poetry; as he puts it, "To drag and break the intonation across the meter as waves first comb and then break stumbling on the shingles" (1965:49). Duncan points out that "the materials of the poem, the vowels and the consonants—are already structured in their resonance, we have only to listen and cooperate with the music we hear" (1973:219), or, quoting Carlyle's "The Hero as Poet," "All speech, even the commonest speech, has something of song in it: not a parish in the world but has its parish accent;—the rhythm or *tune* to which the people there *sing* what they have to say . . . all men have an accent of their own—though they only notice that of others." Just as music is a kind of language, so language is a kind of music. All of these poets have been obsessed, quite characteristically, with verbal music, the music of the English language—as Mallarmé was obsessed with the music of French, and the majority of major Russian poets with that of Russian. Such poets hear music as half or far more than half of the process of making a poem.

Some of this poetic music is universal, free of the uniquenesses of one language: high front vowels such as "ee" practically everywhere connote bright colors and gleeful feelings. Such perceptual universals include "a universal, *Gefühl*-type way of linking experiences, which shows up in laboratory experiments and appears to be independent of language—basically alike for all persons . . . a serial or hierarchical order in the universe" (Whorf 1964:267). But much of the music resonates wholly or entirely within one stock, such as Tarascan or Germanic with their respective vocalic symbolisms, or—perhaps the most extreme case—the musical possibilities of clicks in South African languages. Again, much of the music may be limited to a single language. This underlies the paradoxical opinion of Sapir that "with Heine . . . one is under the impression that the universe speaks German" (Sapir 1921a:240). In other words, the German symbolism—at least for someone with such a native ear—sounds so ideally fitted to the ideas and images in the poem that the hearer comes under the illusion of a total emotional necessity or of an ideal expression. Finally, much of the symbolism is limited to a dialect, and perhaps the best example is not so much the Scots English of Robert Burns, but the inimitable Irishness of the conversation in a well-lubricated Dublin pub.

The music of language, poetic or otherwise, may be blocked off, masked, or simply ignored. Professional literary critics, academic or otherwise, tend to ignore the music of the poems they are reviewing and even the issue of whether and how a poem or poet is musical; the exceptions here such as Hollander are usually poets as well. Most poets—as is often transparent from interviews on their craft—are reticent, inarticulate, cryptic, or astutely devious when it comes to this subject. Some linguistic poeticians have made exciting discoveries that have renovated or could renovate poetry in minor ways: the discovery that the foot as normally understood does not exist in English as a phonetically characterizable entity (the reality being complex beads of energy); or the closely related experiments on so-called isochrony, where, in English, there is "a tendency to squeeze units into relatively equal time spans, marked by chest pulses" (Preminger et al. 1974:408). But the music of language is totally ignored by most poeticians, whose theories cannot differentiate the sound of a great line by Dylan Thomas from a catchy jingle on TV.

The musical imagination underlies all poetry as conventionally defined, where it plays an implicit or potential counterpoint to the rhythm and beat of conversation. This music is a morphology that expresses, not feelings that are too vague for words, but ones that are too precise for words (to adapt the insight of the composer Mendelssohn). In this precision the music of poetry resembles music in the usual sense and differs from other forms of discourse, such as scientific ones, which are less precise emotionally.

The Second Pole: Myth

The second polar process in the imagination involves ideas, theories, and the like—be it the anthropological theories and even methods that underlie some of Eiseley's poems, or the myths and theologies in Sappho, Eliot, and Yeats. For these and other major poets the deeper ideational levels are mythic, or at least multifariously entangled with myth, which is counterpointed to music. Similar myths—or myths interwoven with ideologies, theories, and beliefs—underlie our ordinary conversations about home financing, maturation and adolescent children, the terrors of the national economy, and even last night's baseball game or our theory of chance and probability.

Let me speak of myth, roughly and heuristically, so as, frankly, to satisfy our intuition that something essential is shared by these daily myths and semimyths, as well as by traditional myths such as the Gilgamesh epic, by various mixtures of myth and religion, by master literary myths such as *War and Peace* and *The Divine Comedy*, and by mythologized ideologies such as the revolutionary spirit of France in the 1790s and Russia in 1917–21. Poetry often integrates us with such residues of world myth, ideology, and religion, or with various combinations of them.

How are we to define myth in this heterodox and overlapping sense? For one thing, it displays and sometimes resolves conflicts and oppositions in the culture or the imagination. Often it gives us intimations of powers beyond our control—the mysterious, awesome, sacred, holy, uncanny, spooky, divine, god-saturated, or preternatural, as the case may be: for example, the love-in-nature versus the hatred of natural forces that is a leitmotiv in *Moby Dick*. While the usual vehicle of myth is the narrative line (analogous to the conversational line or the line of a dream), it often condenses emotion, time, and space to an illusion of one point—particularly when embodied in the short lyric.

"Myth" should also be taken to include—as its minimum scope—myths of the unique person. Drawing on the resources of one's being, such unique, individual myth also underlies the image of the self that is symbolized overtly by one's loyalties to place and people, by one's personal routines and impulses, by favorite books, movies, regions, and even foods, and by one's perception of one's traumas and strokes of good fortune. This complex self-myth is multiply projected through sets of alternative egos and shifting poetic and conversational voices. It is through the individual myth-making process that the individual imagination attains integrity with itself and with others in the same culture (or subcultures) seen as wholes.

Myths are translatable partly because they are about universals of experience: biologically, they often involve rudimentary functions or the basic anatomy (the point of departure for so many symbolisms); socially, the family, with its need for cooperation and its ambivalences; emotionally, they play on empathy, curiosity, jealousy, antipathy, hatred, identification, lust, fear, loneliness; they depict universal imaginative experiences of dream, daydream, heightened consciousness, memory, hope, forgetting, sudden realization. On the other hand, the form and content of myth may also be limited to a few cultures or culture areas. The familiar Oedipal tragedy of a son killing his father is clearly analogous to the Irish and South Indian tragedy of a father killing his son—although not a mirror image! Yet other myths are limited to one culture, be this a matter of individual symbols or their qualitative or quantitative arrangement. Quantity becomes quality in the Mesopotamian Ishtar, who, as far as I know, is extraordinary and perhaps unique in the sheer multiplicity of her functions. As a second example, Tolstoy's Pierre Bezukhov does not closely resemble any mythic protagonist before or since.

The universality of mythic protagonists, plots, and themes, then, like the music of language, is a matter of degree of uniqueness. Myth is no more totally translatable than poetry is totally untranslatable; in this I part company with those mythologists who locate myth within a discrete code that is separate from natural language and articulate speech, and, on the other hand, the poets and critics who feel that in some categorical sense, to translate is to traduce. And despite its scope and essentiality for poetry, myth is not, as has been claimed, the master trope of poetry, by which seems to be meant a figure that governs other figures. For one thing, myth is not the "master" of the musical use of language; for another, figures such as image and metaphor may be equally masterful; and finally, myth is perhaps more essential in such universes as religion and even individual psychology.

Let us return to the earlier part of this discussion, because, ideally, the underlying nuances of myth are felt to be somehow consonant with the surface of sound. For example, Sappho is thought to be highly colloquial in many poems, exquisitely expressive of the phonetic nuances of her Lesbian dialect; but, because of universal phonetic-perceptual factors, her poems sound beautiful to someone ignorant of Greek. Concomitantly, her personal myth of Aphrodite incarnates some beliefs of the typical Greek of her time, but also panhuman universals of jealousy, longing, and so forth. To put the matter in clichés, great poetry is rooted in myth, and great myth usually flowers into poetry—just as interesting conversation usually "sounds good." The partly universal aspects of poetry and myth confound certain doctrines of extreme relativism or of linguistic alienation, just as the language-specific aspects of poetry confound the doctrinaire universalist. And there is another, more concrete interdependence: many dazzling semantic-conceptual leaps in poetry are suggested, triggered, and reinforced by a novel alliteration or some other phonic felicity; good examples of this are some of Pindar's mythic associations and Pasternak's philosophical ones.

Let us put the problem in the more comprehensive context of poetic language as a kind of language. Language is the symbolic process that mediates between, on the one hand, ideas/feelings and, on the other hand, the sounds produced by the tongue, larynx, and so forth. Poetry, analogously, is the symbolic process by which the individual mediates between the music of a natural language and the (nuances of) mythic meaning. To create felt consubstantiality between language music and myth *is* the master trope of poetry— "master" because it is superordinate to and in control over such lesser figures as image, metaphor, and paradox. And this master trope is unique, that is, it is diagnostic of poetry.

Poetic Integration, Concluded

Music and myth may be the main components of the master trope, but there are other tropes with scope over the whole poem or conversation that partly constitute its gestalt. In Homer's *Iliad* and *Odyssey* the internal structure of book 1 corresponds roughly to that of book 24, of book 2 to 23, and so forth, in a partially realized version of the as-you-go-in-so-you-come-out figure that is called chiasmus. The same ordering is also elaborated fully if imperfectly within individual books of both poems. In a similar overall process, a poem may resemble a mobile of mirrors that, alluding to other poems and pieces of poems and even to other words in other arts, also interreflect to illuminate and irradiate each other. The most brilliantly constructed of these complex gestalts may be the least obvious and go unnoticed by most hearers and readers, including astute literary critics. Speaking of the alleged lack of organization at these deeper levels of Anna Karenina, Tolstoy said, "I am proud of the architecture. The arches of the vault are brought together in such a way that it is even impossible to notice where the keystone is" (Stenbock-Fermor 1975:8). Poetic language is ultimately a question of the total poem (or conversation), although of syllables and lines as well. This ultimate status of the totality is analogous to the gestalt-level networks of meaning that are said to integrate the grammar and vocabulary of an entire language—in the mind of the native, or at least of a speculative linguist who has tried to go native!

The Poetic Relates to Other Functions and Arts

Granted the importance of tropes, poetic language also depends on functions that are not ipso facto poetic. Poems or other discourse may serve mainly to establish or strengthen contact between parties: love poetry in the conventional language of most love notes. Tone poems are keyed to the linguistic-musical sensitivities of a specific or even specialized audience. Yet other poems depend on focusing on a person in the grammatical sense of *person*: the third person in historical, epic poems; the person addressed—for example, by the persuasive rhetoric of Ulysses; or the speaker or first person, as in the emotive speeches of Achilles. Such person focus often shifts in the course of a poem, or interacts with other functions. In fact, all possible functions in communication are at least implicated in any given act of poetry; moreover, the purely poetic focus cannot work without support from the other functions (Stankiewicz 1979).

The poetic also interdepends with the aesthetic dimensions of such nonverbal arts as the dance, inextricably in many primitive cultures and as an implicit subtext in some modern poets. A similar interdependency may extend to the graphic or plastic arts, as in the many poems about a painting, an architectural structure, or even a pot, as we shall see below. Poetic language, then, is relational, or rather interrelational, to other foci and functions in verbal, quasi-verbal, and nonverbal universes of experience.

Perhaps the primary interdependency relation of poetic language is with the so-called real world—physical, ethical, and above all emotional. The real world of poetry may include such peaceful pursuits as plowing, trading in stocks, playing poker, child care, and softball and baseball. All of these have aesthetic dimensions that can be transmuted into art (Roy Campanella's catching) or into poetic lines about such art (Marianne Moore's line about Campy's catching). But even baseball, with its beanballs and the take-out at second and the collisions at home plate, is partly if often latently violent, and maybe the "really real" of Whitehead boils down to violence and a few similar experiences just as much as to a transcendent religiosity. That death is the ultimate certainty is a truism; but—ask any witness of a natural child delivery—so is birth partly violent, and real through that violence. This violence and disorder in the world interplay with what is partly the same thing, the dangerous powers of the imagination—here, the poet's. It is with violence, as with animal ecstasy, that the poet has been in collusion ever since Homer, ever since the Upper Paleolithic and the birth of song. Listen to Bly (in "The Teeth-Mother") on the use of napalm against Vietnamese peasants:

> If one of those children came toward me with both hands
> in the air, fire rising along both elbows
> I would suddenly go back to my animal brain,
> I would drop on all fours, screaming,
> my vocal chords would turn blue, so would yours.

> (Faas 1978:214–15)

In various ways poems like this help the poet and the reader live with reality. But the felt violence, the violence of the outcry, the metaphysics of violence, and the way violence presses in on us are only extreme demonstrations that poems and the poetic speech of every person—besides being messages about messages, or language about language—are necessarily entangled in other levels of discourse and contexts, including the most problematical one of the "real world." A similar argument would hold for the equally ultimate and impinging reality of human empathy, sympathy, and familial and erotic love, as in my poem, which is based on fieldwork:

Industrial Accident: Mexico

The peasant is pouring insecticide over the arching roots
of young fruit trees in Colima. He can hardly suspect,
sweating from the exertion,
   on his knees, leaning down too low,
     breathing in too deeply—
      that that poison
will filter down in to the tender rootlets of his brain.
Nor does the owner of the plantation
nor his mistress beside him in the afternoon sun
admiring the Indian's biceps, watching him work,
   look ahead to the young wife
beside the living corpse—its twitching—
   later—back in the village.

Intensification is also achieved through a dialogue with the counterfactual, or an unreal love, or a superficially unrealistic violence, as in Blake's "The Tyger":

   Tyger Tyger burning bright,
   In the forests of the night;
   What immortal hand or eye,
   Could frame thy fearful symmetry?

At the moment of creative appreciation and probably of creation, the tiger is not literally visualized and is not transformed into rational, logical, or cognitive messages. The fire, unlike a physical one, burns while it is symmetrical. Conjoining such illogical yet imaginable things speaks to the emotions, just as it is emotion that motivates and employs the mythopoetic imagination.

POETIC LANGUAGE SHAPES THE IMAGINATION

The third part of the relativity hypothesis is that the poetic potential of language—not logic or basic reference—most massively determines the imagination. This idea is found the world over in the so-called native model of folk definitions and folk dichotomies. Many individuals in all societies would agree, if you could make the question clear, that the meanings of their language determine their thinking. Tarascans have told me that Spanish was useful but that they needed Tarascan "to understand things," apparently implying a dichotomy between a Spanish set of labels or signs and a Tarascan language of living symbols. Such native models tend to hold for medicine and other universes that are intricately specific to the culture: magic, myth, religious ritual, and, of course, all the genres of folk literature. But the influence and potential of poetic language interpenetrate all levels and domains, not least those of economy and material culture. As Sapir put it over half a century ago:

> The fact of the matter is that the "real world" is to a large extent unconsciously built up on the language habits of the group. No two languages are ever sufficiently similar to be considered as representing the same social reality. The worlds in which different societies live are distinct worlds, not merely the same world with different labels attached. (Sapir 1951:162)

These well-chosen words have been reprinted in dozens of derivative articles and college texts and quoted or rephrased in thousands of classrooms. But let us go on to the next paragraph in Sapir's statement:

> The understanding of a simple poem, for instance, involves not merely an understanding of single words in their average significance, but a full comprehension of the whole life of the community as it is mirrored in the words, or as it is suggested by their overtones.

Here and elsewhere the author suggests that poems and poetic language provide the strongest case for linguistic relativity.

The conscious ideas of a group, particularly as embodied in religious myth and political ideology, are inseparable from language. Some of the most acute examples of this come from ideologies of ethnic prejudice and national chauvinism. In some cases, prejudice may motivate a plethora of pejorative epithets, such as Wop, Guinea,

Dago, Roman, or Spaghetti-Bender. In other cases a single epithet, such as Kike, does most of the work, perhaps because the ethnic name itself is sufficiently pejorative and stereotypical.

The name for an ethnic group can even be transformed into another part of speech with a partly or wholly independent life, and hence a new, insidious, and constantly infiltrating power, as illustrated by words involving "Jew." In English this word also works as a verb, as in "to Jew somebody out of something." In Russian, after as well as before "The Great October Revolution," a root for "Jew" (*zhid-*) has functioned in a fairly common adjective with pejorative connotations of "mean, poor, run-down, thin, diluted, liquid," as in the ambiguous "the tea is thin" (*chay zhidók*), which can also mean "is Jewish" and even "is like a little Jewish boy." A similar process has led to an identification of the same root for "Jew" with a *third* root, for "stingy." At deep and largely unconscious levels, obviously, these sorts of etymological, grammatical, and semantic processes may feed heavily into ideology and attitudes (here of racism), and vice versa. As Marx and others have argued, even the most completely elaborated ideological representations find their way into language. This can be illustrated by the linguistic reflex of democratic institutions in English political talk/thought, and of communist institutions in the pervasive bureaucratic jargon of Russian. As these ideological representations find their way into language they become subject, not only to habitual classification and grammatical processing, as illustrated, but to analogical transformations of all kinds, ambiguity and marking, the play of tropes, polarization, condensation, and so forth. Thus, as propounded by Lefebvre, "A sociology inspired by Marxism might well address itself to the relations between . . . poetry and myth" (1977:261). Here, however, I would insist on the inadequacy of *any* sociological or heavily sociocentric approach, because the poetic use of language is so largely a matter, not only of society, but of the unique imagination.

Voluminous evidence in support of this third part of the hypothesis, that poetic language shapes the imagination, has been assembled by psychologists, and much has been alluded to in the foregoing discussion concerning poetry in conversation: the proverb among Russians and Africans; the poetic use of single words, including nominally scientific ones; the poetry of swineherds and baseball players; the poetics of obscenity, which may be as fresh as "Jesus, it's like a cow pissing on a flat rock," heard from a trooper as we marched along in a pouring rain.

Better-known examples come from poets, although here it may

be language shaping the poet's imagination *or* the poet's imagination artfully exploiting the structural resources of his/her language. Pushkin's "The Bronze Horseman" associates the two main protagonists with the two halves of a dichotomous verbal category. On the one hand, the colossal, perduring figure of Peter the Great correlates almost exactly with verbs that imply action that is enduring, on-going, continuous, lasting, and so forth. On the other hand, the verbal forms that imply momentary action, whether onset or completion, are correlated just as nearly with the second main protagonist in the poem, an ephemeral, stop-and-start artisan whose sweetheart eventually dies in a flash flood. Here subtle implications of a verbal (so-called aspectual) category are intertwined with contexts to yield a nonobvious but consistent texture (Jakobson 1961). Similarly, in Homer we find an exceptional shifting of verbal (aspectual) categories that imparts a fresh and unpredictable glitter to his epic line.

Turning to Chinese we find that the so-called regulated verse required complex parallelisms of tone and syntax in adjacent lines, combined into a large number of accepted matrices for stanzas. The parallelism also entailed parts of speech and categories of noun by class, color, and shape. In one poem by Tu Fu the successive images in the eight lines run from a new moon to a partly finished ring to (the wall of) a fort to the edge of the evening clouds to the Milky Way to mountain passes to a courtyard to (the corollas of) drenched carnations—all sharing a feature of (the edge of) a semicircle. In a translation of another of Tu Fu's poems, "catkins" parallel "leaves," "lanes" parallel "streams," and "white carpets" parallel "green money":

> The catkins line the lanes
> making white carpets,
> And leaves on lotus streams
> spread like green money.

> (Bly 1973:205)

The parallelisms in categories of shape and other rules of the regulated verse laid down by the Empress Wu, while demanding enough in themselves, are actually of much greater complexity than this discussion suggests. To hit upon appropriate spatial metaphors that fit within the rigorous matrices of the standardized stanzas calls on the deepest levels of a fully developed unconscious—as well as the more or less artful techniques of the linguistic-poetic virtuoso. The role of shape categories in Chinese and the rules for Chinese poetry lead us to the perhaps more extreme case of "shape in grammar"—and in the folk poetry of an American Indian language: Tarascan.

TARASCAN

Of my five years of fieldwork, the majority (1954–56, 1965–67, 1970) have been spent among the Tarascan Indians of southwestern Mexico. I recall watching, sometime in 1967, a young man wander aimlessly in a field at high noon, and then I heard from him that he had been composing a story for me: "The Three Butterflies." This man was a linguistic virtuoso in his aptitudes but also a mad poet in a familiar Spanish or American sense: the most prolific and obscene joker in harvest brigades; the man who knew the most stories in town; whose sentences were the longest and most complex, but whose scores on my tests for Tarascan grammar were the most deviant, and at times wild; who, in a brawl, used the fine, long jacknife I had given him to seriously slash his brother's hand; who, when his mother, a reputed witch, was being buried, leapt down into her grave and stood for a long time on her coffin, apostrophizing her and weeping piteously; who, when I had to go to a neighboring hostile village to get boxes for my wife's pottery collection, led me up the ravines where I would be in the least danger from sniper fire; who overidentified with me and, when I took a different virtuoso back to the States, suffered pathological jealousy and chagrin; finally, a thoroughly *macho* womanizer, who eventually joined the Mexican cavalry, where he did very well. Most Tarascan virtuosi I have known (in ceramics and guitar making as well) had similarly exceptional and emotional imaginations.

This particular story-maker was felt to lack respect for people, within the Tarascan "culture of shame," a complex of attitudes about one's social front, about loss of face—as when, for example, one's face reddens, the skin crawls with shame, one puts on an unshamed mien, or denies that one has witnessed something shameful, or stays indoors for shame, or feels angry or vengeful out of shame, or composes one's features after being shamed. The most powerful verbal symbol in this part of the linguistic culture is, as one would expect, a suffix -ŋaṛi, meaning "face-eye" (see note to Table 1 for the pronunciation of Tarascan symbols). This suffix enters into about fifty complex bases, such as *ambé-ŋaṛi-n*, "to go to pieces, to lose all reputation" (*ambé-*, "to dissolve into particles"). In fact, all the examples just given ("face reddens," and so forth) are rough translations of such Tarascan words. This one suffix combines with hundreds of roots to generate an enormous repertoire, one which our story-maker was quick to use in his back-handed way.

Such virtuosi concoct stories that are passed along from one individual to another in fairly definite form. Their language is special, with introductory and concluding formulae, a fairly fixed form, a studied syntax, and a distinct prosody. The teller of the tale normally will cogitate and recall to himself for a few seconds or minutes before beginning to recite, and there is little variation from one recitation to another by the same virtuoso (as I have checked with tape recordings). The stories shade off in various directions: to other genres, to reports of dreams, and so forth. If apt, they enter the repertoires of the village and region and so become part of the "cultural inventory," in an inclusive and superficial sense. Good stories are learned by nonvirtuosi, such as the young man who knocked on my door one evening to tell me proudly the one story that he knew.

The virtuoso, through his stories, displays an awareness of the body in several ways. Many of his stories are *about* the body: its shape, functions, health and injuries. The body also functions as a general model or point of departure for the most diverse imagery—a sort of anatomical analogue of the world: the long words that include a spatial (usually body-part) suffix are drawn out slowly by the raconteur. They often anchor and/or conclude the narrative line. They are awaited by the listener, often triggering smiles or laughter, and are often repeated in isolation when the story is over.

Many of these words with body-part meanings are constructed by using one of fourteen semantically complex suffixes that occur after the root or base. Each of these suffixes has a primary meaning of a body part or body parts, and then others that are loosely related: an erotic-zone meaning, a house-part meaning, a ceramic meaning, and transferred social and psychological meanings. There is also an abstract meaning that I, as a linguist, could infer and that, although not obvious, seemed acceptable to native speakers.

The "face-eye" symbol, already introduced above, has the additional corporeal meanings of forehead and jaw, and the flat of the chest, stomach, or lower belly, and of the shins, and the erotic-zone meaning of a woman's private parts. The domestic meanings include wall, usually an inside wall but possibly any, if the flattish quality of a wall is to be stressed. The environmental meaning is hillside, cliff face, etc. In a ceramics context, the suffix means the inner side of a pot belly (but the exterior in some circumstances). This suffix is particularly productive in the context of maize, with at least twenty-five "face-eye" stems; and there is a large miscellany of other meanings including sky, types of flap, and so on. In other words, Tarascan "face-eye" is as richly symbolic as English "face," with the additional, abstract meaning of "flatness" and "interiority" and a plentitude of psychological meanings connected with memory and the "shame culture" that stigmatized our virtuoso. Suffixes such as this suggest ways of classifying and even seeing spatial and psychological relations; for example, there are at least five culturally defined ways of crossing one's legs, and some of the labels include the "face-eye" suffix in its meaning of "shin." The Tarascan is more aware than an American of the knee-crossing and -crooking and -stretching of his seated interlocutor.

Let's look briefly at a paraphrase of one Tarascan story, to see how these suffixes work. A mouse emerges suddenly from the kitchen onto the floor next to the wall, for which the suffix for "vertical right angle" is used in one of its domestic meanings. Aunt Onion says that the mouse has a small face, using the root for small plus the "face-eye" suffix. She then speaks boldly or forcefully, which is conveyed by the root *wiŋa-*, followed by the simple body-part suffix for the "jaw-chin-teeth" area. Uncle Peanut's private parts are referred to by one of the several simple corporeal suffixes for the crotch, with the implication here that his penis is hanging out. His bottom is referred to by the slightly archaic word for pants, which contains the complex "bottom" suffix *ču*, as does the following verbal form for having one's clothes torn over one's bottom. The same *ču* serves for Uncle Peanut's penis, which is first stared at by the female cat, then grabbed suddenly and scratched. After a few more lines this rustic tale ends with Aunt Onion asking, "But why should I be mad at the cat?" All of which is funnier in Tarascan than in English. We see, in any case, that suffixes such as "face-eye" and "bottom" cut metaphorically across various domains and zones.

The body-part meaning of these symbols, if it is primary at all, is a sort of first among equals. Corporeal or otherwise, many of the extensions of meaning to the genitals, the parts of a pot, and so forth are unique to Tarascan or to a few other, unconnected languages: for example, our familiar "face-eye" also denoting "shin" and inner surfaces (an ear of maize before it is husked); the back suffix being used for an outer wall or other surface, but also, in mockery, for the shaft of the penis; the neck-throat for a cave; the head for a loft or a gable. Such symbolisms differ from language to language in their organizations and in the degrees to which their specific meanings are predictable on universal grounds, whether these be based on reason or on experience. The fact that many of the classifications and semantic processes are specific to a given language is a cornerstone of the hypothesis of linguistic relativity.

A different insight into Tarascan spatial symbolism comes from a network of associations that I constructed which illustrates the poetic potential of the language and the way spatial tropes organize reality. This is a world where:

> *squash tendrils spread along the ground the way*
> *one passes a stranger suspecting his intentions.*
> *Its rays hit the loins of the distant fields like*
> *someone surveying a far-reaching country, and dry*
> *the dew and hoarfrost off the slopes the way*
> *antipathy congeals between husband and wife.*

These sentences can form the first stanza of a poem in long, loose lines:

Tarascan Country

the sun squints over a ridge and squash tendrils explore an adobe
    wall
  like passing a stranger on an isolated road and suspecting his
    intentions
its rays hit the naked points of distant mountains
  like a lonely man surveying a far-reaching country
drying the dew and hoarfrost on the slopes
  the way antipathy congeals between a husband and a wife.

The rest of the poem runs as follows:

the sky draws fine cirrus and nimbus strata over itself
  a film of ice, the first scab glazing a surface wound
and the tips of a gathering storm cloud blacken like the fruits of a
    cactus
  like gritty fingers touching the dusty butt of a pistol, lightly
after the thunder storm the newly ploughed soil breathes with
    fragrance
  like understanding the elegance in some words by a neighbor
and the borders of fields burst with the pinkness of rain-washed
    poppies
  like women in their embroidered blouses crowding into a patio

orchids hang still and moist from the cypresses and locusts
 as a girl awaits me, her lover, by "the eye of water"
a flock of dark thrushes soars up out of a ravine
 the way I will die in a room or whatever houses me
volcanic ash sifts between the supporting rootlets of the corn
 like inviting friends to a fiesta and receiving them in my
  courtyard

The spatial tropes here are embedded in regular but not frozen forms for long words, with several suffixes. They do appear in conversation and should appear in the dictionary. The almost complete set of forms from my dictionary is given in Table 1.

Let us take a second example. The lingo of the potter might seem lowly or even trivial, but not to anyone who has read the psychological and semantic literature on the vessel as a root or life symbol for the feminine (e.g., Neumann 1972), nor to someone who has experimented with the poetic potential of this universe.

This ceramics lingo in Tarascan implies space and shape, and the pot shape analogizes the body in many ways, some obvious, some subtle: for example, birds (an explicit penis symbol) are not supposed to be painted on the bottom of a pot (a female symbol), whereas a woman can be likened to a pot. Spatial suffixes may refer to parts of pots or other bodies but they also have more abstract meanings: a superior surface resting on an orifice, then the narrowing of a longish object at an intersection followed by a central, bounded area with its own inner surface, and the whole drawing to a close on an underlying zone. It is but a step from such shifting and intersecting geometries and images to a humble poem about ceramic form:

Tarascan Pots

(for Margaret)

I

she marvels at their glossy green:
brilliant moss in sun-flecked water

2

and wonders at their humanness of form
flat tops with covers—hats
over each orifice's flaring lips
the necks, concave and erect

the arm-like handles that arch
from both sides, then in past bulging shoulders
to the continuous, girded globes
of back, paunch, hips
that curve down
to squat bottoms
on which
three feet extended
tripod-like, they sit, solid, fat
yet with a Neolithic simplicity
they feel pregnant with pot-thoughts
expressed on the unseen faces of their red interiors

3

she ponders their designs crowded beneath the glaze

where "circles" are not rims of the moon
the "dots" raindrops, the "meanders" streams

nor the "deer," deer from the sierra
nor the "hills" volcanic sugarloaves to pierce the sky

nor are there "leaves of oak and laurel," nor species of "shell"
but "scallops" and hooked "scrolls" cut from seas and woods

here what we call "deer, hill, leaf, snail, shell, dot, circle
and meander" are merely for the potter's squirrel-tail brush

design units in a world of style
that counterposes elegance against repletion

Routine classifications in Tarascan become, here, the ore for English poems. Similar diffusion is at work today as tens of thousands of American poets and poet-translators creatively transpose from foreign and even exotic traditions into our literary language, converting it, in some imaginations, from an American idiom into a sort of global or interlingual idiom where, at the level of image and figure, ingredients from Chinese, Navajo, medieval German, and hundreds of other sources are suspended, half mixed, or sometimes synthesized into a new compound. But the inverse movement from English outward to the rest of the world is just as possible and just as essen-

Table 1. Tarascan Long Words

Form	Meaning	Verb and Gloss
ȼi	downward, near the ground; lower seen from above	*phikwá-ṛi-ȼi-n*, "to suspect another's intentions" *sirú-ȼi-n*, "to spread on the ground, as of tendrils"
pa	hearth, field, social front	*erá-h-pa-kuṛi-n*, "to survey a sweeping country" *ȼá-h-pa-n*, "to strike a field, as of the sun's rays"
ȼɨ	top, above exterior of upper surface	*ȼirí-h-ȼɨ-n*, "to congeal on a top surface (water, etc.)" *waná-ȼɨ-ku-nta-n*, "to circumambulate a town, as of a band" *wandá-h-ȼɨ-k-pi-n*, "to preach"
ṛu	point, projection of something	*khumá-khumá-ṛu-pu-n*, "to approach and blacken (of clouds, i.e., their tips)" *khumá-ṛu-n*, "to die, as of flowers, fruits"
ndi	ear, shoulder, ground surface, etc.; interior of angle	*phunȼú-phunȼú-h-ku-ndi-n*, "to smell fragrantly, as of soil after a rain" *kuṛá-ndi-n*, "to understand"
nda	around the edge of, on the ground	*čawá-čawá-nda-n*, "to go rapidly along the edge of a field, tearing off cobs, etc." *khutí-khutí-nda-n*, "to circle around something, like robbers" *phaká-phaká-nda-n*, "to push one's way into a crowd"
ŋi	interior, enclosure, cavity	*waŋá-ŋi-ma-n*, "to pass along a ravine" *waṛí-ŋi-n*, "to die inside something (like a chest cavity)"
aṛa	guts, innards; central, bounded	*waṛí-aṛa-n*, "to die inside something, like a womb"

Note: In the table above and elsewhere: *i* stands for a central vowel, *ȼ* for a sound like "ts," *č* for a sound like "ch," *ŋ* for a sound like "ng," *ṛ* for a retroflex flapped *r*, and *h* after a consonant for a slight aspiration (puff of air).

tial to many non-English poets today. Standard classifications that we take for granted are transposed and analogized into parts of new poems in Spanish or Chinese, as they could be in Tarascan—just as, of course, an original flick or tilt will make them input into an English line or fresh discourse.

CONCLUSION

The ways one poet or tradition selects, changes, and transposes from another tests, perhaps most sensitively, the coupled hypotheses of linguistic relativism and poetic indeterminacy. In the first place, the world is uniquely symbolized by a language; and a language, while not substantially the same as poetry, is pervasively poetic. More generally, culture as well as language is a structure in process involving meanings and contexts, and many of the relations among its symbols are analogous in part to poetic figures. It follows that culture itself, of which language is only a fairly obvious part, is, to a significant degree, a work of art. Obviously, then, it is the more artistic universes of this collective work (that is, poetry strictly speaking and the other arts) that most profoundly differentiate languages and cultures—to the extent that they capitalize on these linguistic and cultural uniquenesses. By a seeming paradox, it is also precisely in art that languages are made most accessible to each other, partly because it inspires the virtuoso and the individual response to the virtuoso.

My general argument, synthesizing linguistic relativism and general poetics, is, as stated at the outset, that poetic language is the locus of the most interesting differences between languages and should be studied together with the poetic imagination of the individual. The open, energizing interaction between these two phenomena—the individual and the linguistic—is at the heart of the general hypothesis. Sapir expressed this dialectic and mutual feedback relation very well when he wrote, squarely in the tradition of Herder and Croce, "Language is itself a collective art of expression, a summary of thousands upon thousands [upon millions] of individual intuitions. . . . The language is ready, or can quickly be made ready, to define the artist's individuality [or that of any native speaker]" (1921a:246–47).

4

Indeterminacy in Linguistic Fieldwork

Both intellectual history and systematic argument have indicated
that the interesting differences between languages are mainly located in the areas of nuance, connotation, poetic figure, and the like.
(a) The most obvious evidence for this would appear to come from poetry and poetics and, to a lesser extent, from the poetic strata in conversation, political speeches, and other forms of discourse. Equally
(b) strong evidence, however, comes from many subfields of linguistics,
such as the study of child language, of aphasia and other speech pa-
thologies, and of semantic change over time. But let's look in some
less obvious places.

It has been said that linguistics and poetry are opposite sides of
the same coin, since they come at language (with commensurate intensity) from an analytic, model-conscious angle, on the one hand,
and, on the other hand, from an angle that is synthetic and often
minimally self-conscious, even naive. To supplement the obviously
poetic data in chapter 2 and chapter 7, let's look in this chapter at a
case of purely linguistic, here dialectological, fieldwork. Let's assume, as seems reasonable and may be illustrated by *Huckleberry
Finn* and *The Sun Also Rises*, that the phonetic nuance of variation
between individuals and dialects has a strongly poetic quality and
may become the content or subject matter of highly poetic, phonetic
heteroglossia. Such assumptions about linguistic fieldwork will give
us different eyes for some of our basic questions: about the unique
imagination (e.g., of unusual speakers), the role of the aesthetic in
indeterminacy (e.g., my main helper was an outstanding oral poet

and natural grammarian), and the relation between order and chaos.

First, a bit of general context about the Tarascan area, in the Mexican state of Michoacán. The fifty thousand peasants who speak Tarascan live in villages that range in size from five thousand to a few hundred. Despite real differences between them in wealth and power and the feeling that high-sierra dialects are "better," there is no prestige emulation in the usual sense nor are there centers of linguistic innovation. Every village—and some are very close—has a distinctive dialect that is recognizable in terms of intonation, favored words, and the like; young Tarascans must learn not only to code their own dialect but to distinguish others. All the pueblos are at least partly bilingual in Spanish, although fifteen are still essentially monolingual, and Tarascan is the main (or only) language for most women in the area.

DOING DIALECTOLOGY IN A CHAOS OF DIALECTS

Back in 1955–56 I did fourteen months of partly linguistic fieldwork among the Tarascans, and then in 1966–68 I did over one and a half years of Tarascan linguistics, mainly in the northern village of San José. Despite its small population (about 300) and relative isolation, the village eventually revealed a degree of linguistic inconsistency that not only increased my own sense of indeterminacy as an analyst, but positively boggled my mind. Some of the details are worth recounting.

During the first third of the fieldwork period I relied heavily on a well-known potter, Emilio, partly because he was relatively Hispanicized. Emilio had been raised in San José, as had his deceased father, but his mother was from a village somewhat higher in the sierra to the south and his wife was from the easternmost of a string of Tarascan-speaking villages called the "Eleven Pueblos"; both he and his wife had resided for two years in a nearby mestizo settlement (see figure 1). I also relied to some extent on this man's older brother. One or the other was normally interviewed between 6:00 and 8:00 in the morning—before breakfast and the beginning of pottery activities—and one or the other was often interviewed for an hour in the late afternoon. My former wife's doctoral research was on the ceramics of the town, particularly of Emilio and his wife and oldest son, who form the main subject of her articles on style and creativity. Naturally, we spent considerable time in their household, which adjoined ours.

During the middle half of the field period, I used to record stories one or two hours most afternoons from a fluent and inventive raconteur, a young man in his early twenties called Alberto (whom we met in the preceding chapter). He, too, had been reared in San José, but his wife was from another of the Eleven Pueblos. Moreover, he lived in a joint household with another couple of which the young woman was local but the man from an entirely Tarascan-speaking hamlet; neither this man nor Alberto's wife spoke Spanish at all well. Alberto's three brothers had married mestiza (that is, non-Indian Mexican) women, and one of his brothers refused to speak Tarascan.

The overwhelming bulk of my data and insight in San José were obtained from a man with an unusual memory and sensitivity for words, whom I normally interviewed for two to three hours in the forenoon and noon. Gonzalo, while of San José parentage and upbringing, had lived one year each in a northern region, the central sierra, and the Eleven Pueblos, and he had spent many months in the lake region on religious pilgrimages or commercial trips, selling pottery. His stepmother was from the Eleven Pueblos. His wife was from Ocumicho, immediately adjacent to the south, and he had many social connections there; his daughter also spoke an Ocumicho-derived form of the local dialect. During the first three months of the field trip, we ate our main meal in a yard adjoining Gonzalo's house.

Gonzalo spoke a modified version of Sierra Tarascan; while usually showing n in the position of η (i.e., a back nasal as in English "sing"), his e's and o's were raised in the critical positions, and he had the retroflex shibilant $\acute{s}$ before p and most k positions. Gonzalo also had a fairly conscious awareness of Tarascan, not phonetically but semantically and culturally; for example, he had a precise knowledge of the details of the Ocumicho fiesta cycle—probably the fullest and most complex in the entire area. His daughter's wedding was marked by attention to the social and ritual details, and her courtship itself seemed designed to exemplify all the minutiae of an often arcane and erotic symbolism. Gonzalo's father, a musician, had also lived in many Tarascan towns and was excited about the language (father and son were mainly responsible for the insights in my "Poem of Life," and others). Gonzalo himself was perhaps the most sensitive of the Tarascans I knew and worked with, and a man of signal personal loyalty to his kindred; on parting he gave me a small jar of Tarascan beans "to see if they would take root in Chicago." On the negative side, he suffered from deep emotional stresses, and I am not sure if his unusual control of the meanings of words has lasted.

To sum up, all three of the main experts were primarily speakers of the San José dialect of Tarascan, with the qualification that Gonzalo's speech had many Ocumicho and other outside features. Only Tarascan was spoken in their homes, to the children, and so forth. Yet the immediate phonetic experience of these men involved seven Tarascan pueblos, each with a dialect so distinct that a speaker's origin would be recognized within a few seconds, or at most minutes.

A second indication of the degree of dialectical diversity in San José was the origins of our immediate neighbors. Of the fourteen nearby households, there was only one in which Spanish was spoken, and even here the father and eldest son used Tarascan outside the home, while the mother (who was from a nearby mestizo rancho) "understood nearly everything." In four households Spanish was spoken about half the time. In each case, the father hailed from a mestizo town or one particular local family where Spanish had been preferred, but he also understood much or everything in Tarascan and allowed the mother to use it with the children. One of these fathers was from a mestizo town near the western end of the Eleven Pueblos, but he had learned to understand Tarascan, which was certainly his children's mother tongue in every sense. Of the total of forty adults in the fourteen households, many came from other Tarascan-speaking communities: four from Ocumicho, two from Cocucho, and five from three other towns. Thus, even in the border hamlet of San José, facing out toward the predatory mestizo world, Tarascan was the dominant language, in that in-marrying men were acquiring a passive knowledge and their children were growing up fluent speakers (usually because of the care and instruction of grandmothers). On the other hand, 35 percent of our adult neighbors were from outside communities, and at gatherings such as wakes the mingling of dialects and the switching between Tarascan and Spanish were indeed striking—and confusing.

These diverse origins were part of a communitywide heterogeneity arising, in part, from the fact that many people were related and, to avoid incestuous connections, had to seek spouses from the outside. Of the total of sixty adult women, exactly one-half were immigrants. Seven of these were mestizas, one from a city, and three each from nearby hamlets. Of the twenty-three Tarascan-speaking immigrants, ten were from Ocumicho, three from Cocucho, and nine from seven distinct Tarascan villages. Moreover, fifteen of the Tarascan-speaking women born in San José had (or had had) mothers from four outside, Tarascan-speaking towns—ten had come from Ocumicho. (Obviously, the sets of women and their mothers overlap to some extent, but both accurately indicate the great importance of

Table 2. Bilingualism of San José Women

Tarascan	Spanish	Total
Fluent Tarascan	Little Spanish	15
Fluent Tarascan	Poor Spanish	22
Fluent Tarascan	Fluent Spanish	17
Tarascan understood	Fluent Spanish	2
No Tarascan	Fluent Spanish	4
		60

Ocumicho as a source of dialect influence.) In addition to the gross facts of origin, the approximate levels of linguistic competence are revealing (table 2).

Thus, despite appearances around the plaza and the coordinate bilingualism of most men, the bulk of communication within the home and, in particular, to the children was in Tarascan. As in so much of Indian Mexico, the heartland of the native speech community was the women.

Fieldwork in the midst of such diversity naturally habituates one to phonetic nuances and many kinds of sociolinguistic covariation. The people of San José, moreover, are relatively willing to converse with a beginner, tolerate his errors, and play the language-learning game. On the negative side, the general lack of phonetic consistency in my interlocutors was coupled with certain particularly variable features in the speech of many individuals, notably the loss of aspiration (h) in the affricates (ϕ and $\check{c}$, that is, "ts" and "ch"), and the merger of the back nasal η, when it occurred between vowels, with the regular nasal n; these and other details became a source of considerable difficulty in inferring the phonology—and of some personal anxiety as well.

It was with some relief, after nine months in and out of Tarasco, mainly San José, that I welcomed the opportunity to interview two recognized story-tellers from Cocucho, a town high on the flank of a mountain of the same name situated about four hours away to the south, deep in the Tarascan Sierra. Cocucho is notoriously ethnocentric, with only one in-dwelling mestizo (a woman who married into the community), and was the victor in a drawn-out border conflict over some rich valley land that resulted in many fatalities for the opposing community. One of the two visitors was particularly well-known in San José because he had won a New Year's Day storytelling contest several years earlier and because he had married a girl from one of the most conservative Tarascan-speaking families, whose mother, in turn, was from Cocucho; otherwise, he had never lived outside Cocucho, had had only two years of schooling there, and was not too fluent in Spanish.

From the first it was clear that this man, Feliciano, stood in a very sensitive relation to Tarascan; he tended, for example, to correct my placement of the back (i.e., dorso-velar) $ŋ$ and the retroflex $ś$, as well as my intonation, and to point out various syntactic ineptitudes. He was also the sort who can turn a phrase or shift an intonation in a way that refreshes the conversation. Later it became clear that he was singularly certain about the language as a system and about his own control and, with some encouragement, was competent to discuss diverse aspects of its inner form. Like Gonzalo, he was interested in conservative or archaic ritual—in carving masks, in making *khwerékwa* pots, and in the details of the traditional dances.

On his second visit to San José, a three-day sojourn, I walked him down the almost impassably muddy road to the county seat and then went on to the regional capital, where we reviewed my entire list of Tarascan base roots, checking, in particular, the placement of $ŋ$ and the retroflex flap $ṛ$. Thereafter the people in San José affirmed that I spoke like someone from Cocucho, and this was correct because I had been "converted," as it were, to Feliciano's village dialect. During the fall of 1967, Feliciano came to San José on several occasions for three days and we visited him in Cocucho, but most of the time I continued to interview in San José, mainly with Gonzalo, who was still the best man for words and lexical semantics; together we reviewed Gilberti's sixteenth-century dictionary with great care.

In December 1967, I picked up Feliciano in Cocucho and brought him back to Chicago. For three months he was interviewed two or three hours a day, resulting in fourteen excellent tapes of sentences and stories and a dictionary of roots and derivations (cross-checked against the San José dictionary), together with much other data. Some of the interviewing was of the most intensive, paradigmatic sort, often grueling and taken to great lengths and depths. We had actually been speaking only Tarascan from our first conversation in San José, but the sojourn in Chicago gave us a chance to define and discuss all the basic symbols in terms of other symbols in the same system and to talk over the details of the language, as well as to use the resources of the language in new contexts. Feliciano also participated in the first version of my course on the structure of Tarascan. It is the Feliciano Santiago corpus, particularly the eleven tapes, which have been reviewed many times, that has served as the main empirical basis for my phonology and the main point of reference and support for the discussions of variation. Obviously, *complete* homogeneity or consistency is not assumed for Feliciano's speech, much less for that of Cocucho.

During August, September, and most of October 1970, two years after returning to Chicago, I was back again in Michoacán and carried out a fairly comprehensive dialect survey, visiting twenty-six pueblos (but not Cocucho). This greatly widened my phonological horizon and led to numerous improvements in the analysis, particularly the better identification of idiosyncratic and dialectal factors.

To conclude, when my own still-changing and insecure Tarascan confronted the extraordinary levels of individual variation in San José, the result was increased indeterminacy—both as observer-analyst and as poet responding to the rhythms and imagery. As the most feasible solution, I settled for *one* poetic but consistent speaker from a *different* but related community and used the facts of variation as a source of insight into the (pan-Tarascan) system as a whole. While the degree of variation was great, it was less than would be encountered by a Tarascan linguist studying the 108 units in my Chicago apartment house, which represent fifty-one national origins, and how many states of the Union—and whose English?

FROM A CHAOS OF DIALECTS TO A DIALECTOLOGICAL STRUCTURE

The disconcerting degree of variation in tiny San José inspired me to return, confront stubbornly, and figure out at least some of the underlying system (as I had returned in 1966 to figure out the system underlying the suffixes that intrigued and puzzled me in 1955–56). Almost three years later, in September 1970, I did return for three months of fieldwork that, together with what I had collected earlier and what had been reported on three pueblos by Attinasi, Foster, and Swadesh, gave me good, comparable data on twenty-six pueblos (about half the total) of the Tarascan area. This included pueblos known to have highly distinctive sound systems, some of them on or even beyond the perimeter, some of them deep in the mountains.

I always started by bus from Pátzcuaro, but eventually the pueblos had to be reached by foot and/or some third-class bus. The interviews lasted one to three (usually two) hours and involved fifty

Figure 1. Tarascan Towns (Adapted from West 1948)

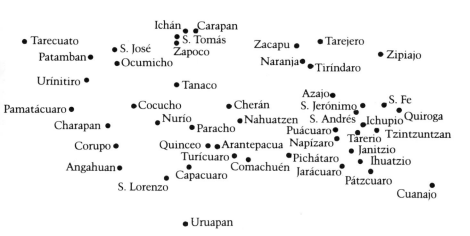

to 130 key words, most of them contextualized in one or several utterances. The interviews were generally in Spanish to keep the speakers from imitating my particular Sierra Tarascan, although, precisely because of my accent, they tended to shift to Tarascan in sierra towns. Most interviews were, by my stated preference, with two speakers or even a small group (to control against individual variation), and were conducted in rooms, porches, and the backyards of peasant homes. For mnemonic-organizational reasons I never did more than one dialect a day (it was fruitful to spend the next day or two after an interview reviewing my notes and thinking about the results). Eight towns were revisited for double-checking. (See figure 1 for a map of the Tarascan area.)

The resulting dialectology is one of the most complete for a New World language and includes solutions to many parts of the vowel and consonant system. But I must limit myself here to a fascinating segment of the vowel system. For the sake of the general reader, I will abbreviate considerably and simplify the vocabulary; for example, the reader is referred to the original publications (see the bibliography) for the details on the sets of "shibboleths" used in the study. In what follows I will consider the vowels along two dimensions: first, the changes that have transpired since the sixteenth century, when Maturino Gilberti published his great dictionary; second, the contrasts between pueblos "today," that is, in 1970.

The main kinds of variation in the vowels involve *e* and *o*. The variation is revealed in two critical positions: first, in suffixes; second, in the unstressed first syllable of a considerable number of non-suffixal or "base" roots. Such base roots are nominal or verbal in a relative sense only, that is, any nominal root can be minimally verbalized and any verbal root can be nominalized, in either case through the appropriate suffixation.

There is one across-the-board generalization: suffixes that were pronounced with an *o* in the sixteenth century today have a *u*, as in *ndu* "base, foot" or *nu* "patio, bottom." The vestigial exceptions need not detain us here.

In the base roots, on the other hand, the old *o* is maintained today in about half the dialects; the most diagnostic position for this is base roots with the shape *Coṛé-* (where C stands for any consonant); for example, the base root *huṛé-* or *hoṛé-* "to learn, be able," or the word for "Tarascan, Indian," which is *poṛé*. For the purposes of blocking off dialect regions and ordering sound changes, it is necessary to distinguish between dialects that only shift *o* in the canonical form *Coṛé* and those that shift it in all the relevant positions. The nominal roots that show these dialectal differences include *apó-pu* "prickly pear" (where -*pu* is a suffix) and *hapó-nda* "lake" (where -*nda* is a suffix).

The widespread shift of the back *o* to *u* in base roots that I have just sketched is partially paralleled by the merger in some dialects of the front *e* to *i*. This complementary process, again, usually involves a regular or total shift in the suffixes; for example, *me* "edge-orifice, oral" or *pe* "plural object, benefactive." This situation of merger contrasts with that of the base roots, where it is limited to some forms with the shape *eCV́*, such as *etú-kwa* "salt" (versus *itú-kwa*). In the case of some radically shifted dialects, however, the shift from *e* to *i* is not limited to some (sets of) bases but takes place in any initial unstressed position.

Let me sum up the dialectal variation in vowels. About a third of the pueblos, all of them in the Sierra, display a general raising, that is, a merger of *e* with *i* and of *o* with *u*. Since the shift of *o* to *u* in suffixes is pan-Tarascan, this leaves us with three slots of diagnostic value: first, *e* to *i* in suffixes; second, *e* to *i* in base roots; third, *o* to *u* in base roots. So the formula for these Sierra dialects is *i/i/u*. San José belongs to this Sierra set.

Figure 2. Tarascan Dialect Structure

With two exceptions (discussed elsewhere), all of the logically possible combinations actually occur ($2^3 = 8 - 2 = 6$), as is displayed on the following matrix list of sets; since the vocalic combinations correspond almost exactly to regional geographical divisions, they have been so labeled.

	1	2	3	4	5	6
1. Suffix *e* to *i*	✔			✔	✔	✔
2. Root *o* to *u*		✔			✔	✔
3. Root *e* to *i*			✔	✔		✔

    1. Eastern: Zipiajo, Ihuatsio
    2. Northeastern Lake: Azajo, S. Fe
    3. Eastern Lake: Ichupio, Cuanajo
    4. Western Lake, some Sierra: Tarecuato, Cherán, Pichátaro, Cocucho, Puácuaro, Jarácuaro, S. Jerónimo, Patamban, Comachuén
    5. Eleven Pueblos: Zapoco, S. Tomás
    6. Major Sierra: S. José, Ocumicho, Tiríndaro, Quinceo, Capacuaro, Angahuan, S. Lorenzo, Pamatácuaro

At the other extreme, a third of the towns have shifted in only one position. Two eastern pueblos have only shifted the *e* in suffixes, giving a formula of *i/e/o*. Two others in the northern lake area have only shifted the *o* in base roots, giving an *e/e/u* formula. Two far-eastern pueblos have only shifted the *e* in base roots, yielding *e/i/o*.

The final third of the pueblos is intermediate between the western Sierra and the eastern lacustrine extreme, having shifted in two of the three diagnostic positions. These major intermediate types include the Eleven Pueblos, which only retain the *e* in base roots, giving a formula of *i/e/u*. In the second place, many Sierra towns such as Cocucho retain the *o* in base roots but have raised all the *e*'s, resulting in an *i/i/o* formula.

Vocalic variation shows the Sierra to be innovative, with maximum variation farthest to the west, while the northern and eastern lake regions are conservative, with maximum conservatism farthest to the east. There remain certain patterns that hold for the entire area. Nowhere is there a pattern of raised vowels in base roots combined with a retained *e* in suffixes. No pueblo preserves the maximally conservative possibility of mid vowels in all positions. Every-

Table 3. Tarascan Child Bilingualism

1. Essentially monolingual Tarascan:
   Azajo, Quinceo, Urapicho, Zapoco, S. Tomás, Ichán, S. Fe, Zipiajo,
   Cocucho, Ocumicho, Capacuaro, Angahuan, S. Lorenzo, Puácuaro,
   the islands except Jarácuaro
2. Primary competence in Tarascan, considerable Spanish:
   Cuanajo, Tarecuato, Carapan, Comachuén, Nurío, one barrio of
   Pichátaro
3. Competence in both Tarascan and Spanish:
   San José-Ocumicho
4. Primary competence in Spanish, considerable Tarascan:
   Ichúpio, Cherán, Ihuatsio, Jarácuaro, one barrio of Pichátaro
5. Essentially monolingual Spanish:
   Naranja, Tarejero, Patamban, Charapan

where the *o* is raised to *u* in suffixes (as already noted). The overall structure is summarized in figure 2.

The personal coda to this analysis is that at some time during the 1970 fieldwork I had assembled parts of the structure and realized where it was heading; from then on my visits to individual pueblos were attended by mounting expectations that all the pueblos would fall into one encompassing paradigm, or that some larger paradigm would emerge. Once my former wife and I walked for some time through the sierra to Zirahuen, only to learn that it no longer had any Tarascan speakers (as, indeed, West [1948] had stated after his fieldwork in the 1940s). But at some point in November, I reached a pueblo that did complete the paradigm; the final month of additional visits confirmed a discovery of vowel and consonantal structures that were often pan-Tarascan and that, of course, neatly accommodated (almost) all the chaotic variation that had so maddened me in San José.

Of great interest is the degree of bilingualism in children of about five or six, before school influences. The main variants are set out in table 3.

The Poetry of Language in the Politics of Dreams

Dreams, as a kind of communication, are also a kind of language or, better, are partly constituted by a stratum that should be called a language: a system of recurrent, meaningful, cultural, partly verbal symbols that are affective, cognitive, and referential. But this "language of dreams" is also a metaphor of language in the usual sense: for one thing, the immediate function and intent of dreams is centered within one imagination rather than between a plurality of speakers (e.g., many generalities about language as essentially a discourse phenomenon simply do not hold here); for another thing, while dreams often include words and sentences, they are primarily visual rather than verbal in their content; for yet another, "the poetry of dreams," in the sense of the frequency and salience of specific figures, differs significantly from the poetry of ordinary language. Rather than leading us to ignore dreams, it is this exaggerated self-centeredness, minimal verbalness, and basically different aesthetics that make dreams a limiting case in the study of language in general and of poetic language in particular.

The study of dreams illuminates other major problems dealt with in this book. One of the most general properties of dreams is their fluidity, their flow, their general looseness. They seem to arise from a vague matrix sea, a sort of nowhere, to which they return unless they are interrupted by the dreamer waking up or they pass by association into other fleeting shapes. Thus, of all forms of communication, dreams, including daydreams, are, if not chaotic, then at least related in the most direct way possible to the world of chaos and indeterminacy in the unconscious. For these reasons it is decisive that even the swirl of dreams is significantly structured in the sense of having units (termed "oneiremes" below) with patterns of hierarchical organization and linear association that, incidentally, are strongly aesthetic in form and goal. The reality of dreams, which hangs over the abyss of the unknown, is partly knowable through dream language.

In the essay that follows I will argue that the primary significance of many dreams derives from the present situation of the dreamer in the world—family, work, local and world politics. The discussion is first grounded in my experience with studying my own dreams. I then give the text of a sample dream and interpret it in terms of both personal symbols and the sort of information that would be brought to it by a typical public (e.g., college-educated, with some knowledge of psychoanalysis). This is followed by a sketch of a model for interpreting the language of dreams and, within this, a model of the essentials of the poetry of that language. The dream model emphasizes the complexity of the dreamer's poetic and other symbolic processes or strategies and of their complex, multimedia nature. Using this model I then reinterpret the political significance of the long sample text. Some of the advantages of nonreductive interpretations are suggested. Without reducing them to a single theory or two, treating dreams (prose or otherwise) in terms of poetic language and political context gives us both a new kind of notation for transcribing them and a valuable source of insight into their nature.

EXPERIENCE AND DATA

I think that a theory of dreams is made more valid if interpretation is anchored to a considerable extent in unique dreams, including those of the theorist. We need such direct connections between theory and data. Let us observe the river of dreams and try to perceive how the poetic stratum within them works. In other words, I want rigor, as illustrated below, but not at the cost of neglecting the texture of dreams or their functions in the dreamer's so-called real world, which includes intrapsychic and depth elements as well as the economic and political conflicts that surround us.

This paper emerges from an on-going exploration of the problems of alienation and personal involvement and commitment (and other kinds of subjectivity) in my twin disciplines of cultural an-thropology and linguistics—both partly wedded to my third profes-sion, poetry. As for raw materials, I have always been a great dreamer and have been habituated to reporting and sometimes analyzing my dreams with relatives, particularly my wife Deborah. It was Deborah who persuaded me to take them seriously enough to jot down notes on 116 of them over a five-year period (1977–1982). Usually this was within seconds after waking up, or during the same day, or, when the dream was exceptionally vivid, during the immediately following days (never more than a week later). These recording practices were partly determined by the great mnemonic differences between dreams—from those which you can barely grab the fleeting end of as you wake up to those which are so vivid and, at times, traumatic that they are recalled with details years later. The dreams, in any case, were written out in full from notes in the fall and winter of 1982–83; and a one-hour talk (that included five dream texts) was given at a Jung Institute and at the University of Chicago in the spring of 1983. About three dozen of the longer and more interesting dreams were also rewritten in the spring of 1983.

I strove for total accuracy in the first typescript, but soon be-came intrigued by the way these dreams were poetic. I began to re-write them as poems—playing with types of line, listening for rhythms, and so forth. However, I always felt that their essential content and structure were in the hands of what I facetiously called "the master down there." He would condone some adumbrations, ex-tensions, or cuttings (e.g., that my hat was floppy "like Walt Whit-man's"—which simile I did *not* dream); but he would reject cate-gorically what he felt were substantive changes. After years in the relatively permissive milieu of poetry, where almost anything goes, this chthonic master came as a relief of sorts.

Accepting this daemon, on the other hand, leaves one with three alternative kinds of text. First, the transcripts of dreams that for all their poetry in terms of image, metonym, and other tropes are still essentially prose; second, the poems that could be spun (or pounded) from dream texts but that, mainly for the sake of verbal form, depart substantively from them; last, dreams that *are* poems, that is, the exceptional dream that has or falls naturally into a meter, a rhythm, a series of lines, or some combination of criteria that satisfy a nar-row definition. Ultimately, this is a matter of degree, with dreams that range from the banal and repetitive (which, however, always have some poetry) to dreaming a realized poem à la Coleridge and *Kubla Khan* (I have dreamt poems but couldn't bring the product back).

The output from five years of "data collection" and a few months of write-up was the 116 texts mentioned above, many of them "banal and repetitive," and about thirty-five prose pieces of some poetic interest. As of 1983 one text had emerged as a realized poem according to a diverse set of editors, poets, and critics (and was selected by the editors of *Dreamworks* from among five others of mine for publication later this year—see "First Draft" below). Let us now leap directly "into the middle of things," with a transcription of one dream that is short, vivid, typical, and relatively accessible.

TEXT

Gangs of young toughs are cruising deserted streets pelting each other with pieces of keen-edged, abrasive quartz. I am one of them and I quit—an insult. Quartz cuts my kneecap and I turn into the paved courtyard of a synagogue and through tunnel corridors to the major room hung about with paintings—orange and green, loud colors on white—and a youngish artist in a yarmulke. He begs me to judge them and I do and saunter out again like Walt Whitman in his floppy hat onto Italianate squares and uneven bending streets lined with sycamores and telephone poles aslant, with single wires—the hooligans watching from a distance. A green heron—the green of earth, greener than green, which I call "Sharonne"—starts up out of a different hardwood to perch on a wire and a stone cracks its wing. It flits up, then swerves back to the corrugated bark of the locust tree to cling and claw, and then drops straight to me. It tips its head to one side, it flaps. I am weeping with outrage as I peg rock after rock at the gang fleeing in all directions down and off the street.

PERSONAL INTERPRETATION

This dream seems to reflect my conflict-ridden experiences of achieving acceptance in peer groups that I saw as tough and where there was in fact considerable ambivalence—mutual affection laced with suspicion and competitiveness. The main instances of this central, organizing fact were my Irish-American high-school classmates in athletics and farmwork, the foreman and his two sons on my father's Vermont farm, ethnic buddy groups in the paratroopers, and certain categories of scholars, notably Indo-Europeanists. I made all these teams, at a cost.

Quartz abounded on our family farm and merges here with other kinds of stone and crystal, notably from the poetry of the Russian Jew, Mandelstam.

The yarmulke is associated for me with regulated, scholarly activities, and a socioreligious sense of appropriateness: German and Yiddish *Sittlichkeit*. It contrasts metaphorically with the floppy hat of Walt Whitman, suggestive of freedom and the open road, and his "I wear my hat as I please" (one of my father's favorite lines).

Deserted, cobblestoned streets, plazas, courtyards, and the like— all frequent in my dream inventory—reflect much travel in Europe and Mexico and, despite relatively long sojourns in the latter country, are most often identifiable as Italian.

The heron seems to stand for many visionary female sightings— particularly the Little Green Herons that, like visiting female spirits, keep watch over the east lagoon outside Hyde Park, where I have lived over twenty years. But even more they stand for many traumas with dying birds (the subject of many of my poems)—the blue heron found frozen by the Concord River, a huge crow found dying of poison, a dead loon by Lake Michigan, and a migratory Canada Goose whose wing was capriciously broken by a ten-year-old boy with a rock.[1]

Let us return to other master symbols. Honey locusts dominate the flora of Hyde Park and are confused in my imagination with the locusts and willows of Concord and Mexico.

The pervasive green mirrors the greens of Vermont, and of Mexico after the rains, the extraordinarily brilliant green glaze of the Mexican ceramics that my former wife analyzed for her thesis, the "green green" of a Wallace Stevens poem, the green in Lorca's main poem, "green I want you, green, green," and also the scientific problem of green and blue-green on which my colleagues have expended so much thought; last, the green of Ireland so important to my high-school friends, versus the Jewish orange of the oranges that they threw around on St. Patrick's Day. So goes some of the experiential input to this symbol.

As for the painter in the dream, my wife is Jewish and an exhibited painter, a published poet, and a semiprofessional singer—an artist in a strong sense of the word—who often asks me for opinions of her work; we identify with each other. The dream also reflects my identification with Whitman and with the model of the poet as a fighter for freedom, specifically the freedom of language that is so important in Russia (e.g., Pushkin, Akhamatova).

At a deeper level, the dream implies my identification with my only son, who at the time was both a sensitive art student and a street-wise New Yorker with an aviator's jacket, switchblade, and Puerto Rican gang friends; his imagined death by a switchblade is the subject of a poem.

The name Sharonne reminds me of the almost intolerably green green—usually in the chartreuse-turquoise area—of some of my formal, that is, chromatic and geometrical, dreams. But I am left with a sense of mystery about this name and its color, which I will explore below.

The above is the sort of crucial personal information that you need to get inside the dreamer's dream—unless you are willing to cut the dream off from the dreamer.

GENERAL, PUBLIC MEANINGS

Let us turn from avowedly personal, anecdotal, and yet indispensable background facts to the general meanings that almost any contemporary American intellectual would bring to a reading of the dream—noting, for example, the Christian nature of the image of "paintings in a sanctuary." There is clearly a felt danger of pop culture and philistine attitudes toward culture and a sense of outrage at the violence in our streets. Pieces of quartz, cobblestones, brickbats, and the like are associated with whatever can cut kneecaps, heads, yarmulkes, birds' wings, and other phallic symbols. They are implements of castration or at least of male genital mutilation. This concrete castration, so to speak, is an analogue of a more comprehensive liquidation—of art, poetry, beautiful birds, Jews, and other cultural and natural values that need to be protected by the fighter-poet. The dream appears to define and in some sense heal the self of the dreamer by creating a vivid image of a semisexual entry into a realm of art and beauty. The chartreuse-turquoise green with its mysterious name seems to emerge as an absolute value that stands for itself more than it symbolizes something else. But what dimensions of analysis can we use to reach a more precise and penetrating interpretation?

THE STRUCTURES-IN-PROCESS

The things just discussed are public as well as private matters—hence the essential communicativeness of dreams, the egalitarian way, even, that they can transcend differences in class and ethnicity.

But in addition to the vague and universal values of colors such as green (or green-blue), objects such as stone, and feelings such as identification and guilt, dreams are also constituted by structures-in-process. Incidentally, while critical of structuralism as a school, I am even more critical of antistructuralism; one needs units and structures for discussion and analysis—and always has them, if only by virtue of the necessity of using natural language.

The simplest such structures are the minimal units that recur as regular components in a set of dreams—preferably a fairly large one. By "minimal" I mean that, for example, "stone" could consist of two components such as "outside surface" and "interior," but in fact never does. These regular components in a person's dreams, these *dream atoms* may, depending on the dreamer, run from a few score to a few hundred or even thousand (the upper limit has never been established but might approximate the number of motifs in an index of folklore). Dream atoms such as primary colors, the low integers, or universal natural phenomena are not a closed set but may be variously modified; just as "moon" is connotatively masculine in German, so it could become masculine or androgynous in some individual system. The crucial stipulation is that these atoms reflect individual or cultural experience and that they are neither genetic in origin nor necessarily generic in classification: an atom can be a unique person (e.g., Stalin), place, name, action, state, phrase, or abstract idea, whatever—the sort of thing that is named by a proper noun or qualified by a date.

The set of atoms in the imagination of the dreamer is partly recreated every night. The atoms are combined to such an extent that some dreams may seem to be composed entirely of previously dreamt material; one doesn't even bother to record them (obviously a mistake in terms of some ideal scientific recording systems). One often reworks one or more dreams in this way. There is indeed a tendency to redream as one gets older and more self-conscious, until some dreams consist primarily of recycled material (just as poets tend to write more and more about their own earlier poems). Such redreaming may involve refinement of meanings and a deepening of one's understanding as the imagination seeks to solve a problem or at least to clarify a profoundly unsolvable one. In "Sharonne" (figure 3) the (images of) gangs of toughs, cobblestoned streets, strong green, and so forth are all atoms in my system. I recognize that dream atoms are not necessarily the only crucial elements: witness the heron and the name "Sharonne" in this dream. I will use the term "oneireme" both for atoms and for nonrecurrent elements (the latter symbolizing some of the indeterminacy in the phenomenon).

Let me try to ground the definition of oneiremes in two ways. First, in the text of "Sharonne" (below) I have bracketed all the atoms that either recur in other dreams in my sample of texts, or that, as far as I can recall, recur as part of my "dream inventory." I have circled elements that are probably atoms. Atoms as a whole are tabulated in table 4 in terms of four levels: 1) the general, superclass, then 2) generic atoms, then 3) specific atoms that occur in "Sharonne" and elsewhere, and finally, 4) related atoms that I feel could occur in another dream of mine; note that some potential atoms probably would not occur, notably an Arabic poet, a Sandhill Crane, the KKK, an elbow, or a eucalyptus tree.

Dream atoms cluster into two more complex kinds of oneireme: the association and the formula. Formulae may be verbal, musical, or even complexly mathematical; but more typical are subtle analogues to verbal sequences that range in size from a single, contextually identified syllable to an imagistic phrase such as "sycamores lining cobblestoned streets" to the equivalent of an entire text that is pages in length. An oneiric association, on the other hand, may be as simple as the dyad "green and Irish" (or Islam), but usually is built into more dynamic, multidimensional entities that resemble, not the compounds of the chemistry lecture, but the elements themselves as they combine during catalysis, that suddenly synthesize and interrelate orange and green, Jew and Arab, artist and fascist. Both formulae and associations tend to operate within one domain such as music or natural language, rather than between such domains.

Oneiric associations control "Sharonne" to some extent; for example [[streets—courtyards—squares] [deserted, cobblestoned]]. Other associations, on the other hand, while seemingly "natural," do not recur in any of my dreams; [orange-Jew] would be a case in point. As the dream progresses there are many new, non-atomic elements that I have never dreamt of before or since (e.g., remembered or recorded)—the yarmulke, a floppy hat, the heron, and, above all the name "Sharonne." There are also many new associations and formulae as the dream advances, in contrast to the opening scenario, which, for me as for most persons, consists almost entirely of dream atoms in well-known combinations—here phrases of two or more atoms that can be bracketed. Other such standard scenarios for me are a formal dance on a parquet floor and an extended family reunion on a New England farm.

Figure 3. "Sharonne"

[[Gangs of young toughs] are [cruising]] [[deserted] streets] [pelting] each other with (pieces) of (keen-edged,) (abrasive) [quartz]. [I am one of them] and [I quit]—an [insult]. Quartz [cuts] my [kneecap] and I [turn into] the [[paved] courtyard] of a [synagogue] and through [tunnel] [corridors] to the [major room] (hung) about with (paintings)—[orange] and [green], (loud colors on white) —and a [youngish artist] in a yarmulke. He begs me to [judge] them and I do and [saunter] out again like Walt Whitman in his floppy hat onto [[Italianate] squares] and (uneven) [[[bending] streets] lined] with [sycamores] and [telephone poles] aslant, with (single wires)—the [hooligans] watching from a distance. A [[green] heron]—the [green of earth], [greener than green], which I [call] "Sharonne"—[starts up] out of a different hardwood to [[perch] on a wire] and a [stone] [cracks] its [wing]. It (flits up,) then (swerves back) to the [[corrugated bark] of the locust] tree to (cling and claw,) and then [drops straight] to me. It tips its head to one side, it [flaps]. I am [weeping with outrage] as I peg [rock] after rock at the [gang] [fleeing] (in all directions) down and off the [street].

Table 4. *Dream Atoms*

Superclass	Generic	"Sharonne" Atom (particular to this dream)	Related Atom (related to other dreams)
group	gang	young toughs	Blackshirts
building	religious building	synagogue	Catholic cathedral
body	extremity	kneecap	hand
stone	rock	cobblestone	pebble
thoroughfare	street	square	dirt road
tree	locust	honey locust	black locust

BOUNDARIES AND CONSTRAINTS

What I hope are suggestive speculations on the practically infinite scope and depth of the oneiric imagination also raise in acute form the question of how it is bounded and constrained. The atoms, formulae, and associations are, in the first place, not bounded in several of the ways that dominate in other kinds of symbolic activity—notably the here-and-now of the speech situation. This particular difference, incidentally, makes irrelevant or subject to heavy qualification much of the apparatus of linguistics, since in the dream the addresser equals the addressee, and, moreover, the trivium of syntax, semantics, and pragmatics collapses into one structure-in-process. Even neurolinguistic variables bound language differently in dreams. Yet despite these qualifications, dreams involve a code of sorts that works within two bounded universes.

The boundaries that seem relevant to the analysis are two: the dreamer's imagination and, as a subset of that, his/her culture. The imagination includes as its input biographical details such as a newsflash from Lebanon the preceding day that may key a dream, together with all other unique experiences along the path back to infancy that are remembered or at least have some potentially active function in the dreamer's imagination. But, more generally, the imagination includes all processes by which the individual integrates knowledge, perceptions, and emotions. It includes attitudes, values, and other symbolic entities, the individual's theory of dreams, and what might be called dream style; the above dream illustrates my own vivid, cinematic dream style, with many well-organized details, notably colors, and a synthesis of the extremely personal with what might be called the cross-cultural or anthropological. The imagination is bounded only by the information received during one's life and one's mental resources for dealing with it—another reason for basing a theory of dreams—at least in part—on the theorist's own dreams.

The second bounding and controlling universe is the symbolism of the dreamer's culture. And it is perhaps dreams more than any other experience that make it possible to cut sharply along the belabored line dividing what is cultural and symbolic from what is behavioral. To paraphrase my definition in chapter 3, culture is an open, constantly evolving, and goal-oriented system of meanings, values, symbols, and emotional patterns that are shared and transmitted by the members of a society. It is true that the form and content of Navajo dreams shade by degrees via marginal Navajo-Americans into the dreams of ethnic factory workers and on into the world of Woody Allen and the syncretic multicultural universe reflected above in "Sharonne." Nevertheless, despite the variety and continuity of cultural universes from an observer's perspective—the eye of the high-flying comparativist—the cultural universe of any one individual is almost as clearly bounded as that individual's biography and personality. Cultural systems, in this sense, are subsystems of individual systems that draw on cultures seen in the usual way at the social level. I have been struck by how dream psychologists ignore cultural boundaries; Freud's "Wolf Boy," for example, was of Russian parentage and bilingual in Russian and German, but the implications of this massive cultural constraint, so crucial for symbols like "wolf" and "butterfly" (really "butterfly-moth"), are almost totally ignored or passed over in silence.

The shunning of cultural meanings, as of biography in a systematic sense, is the effect as well as the cause, cybernetically, of a universalist bias in dream interpretation. I would grant and indeed emphasize the role of universals in dream life. This can be genetic universals such as the fear of falling from a height (as the heron did). It can also be what I call "universals of experience" above (chapter 3); these involve the human body, basic kinship relations, basic natural things such as stone, basic emotions such as jealousy-envy, and basic experiences such as dreaming. But from the point of view of the dreamer, which is the most important point of view and one we are constantly striving to enter, this differential universality is irrelevant, as are the cultural systems of what I called the high-flying comparativist. The system of meanings and emotions organized by the individual is a complex analogue of the system of meanings organized by a culture.

THE POETRY OF LANGUAGE: THE PLAY OF POIESEMES

The structures-in-process of oneiric atom, formula, and association are the constituent symbols for a poetic language, that is, textures and integrations of sound and meaning that call attention to themselves in terms of the aesthetic canons of the dreamer's culture. Poetic language in this sense means, not specific phonological devices, but two dozen or more ways that oneiremes are combined and transmuted. To avoid the connotational baggage of "figure" and "trope," I will coin the term "poieseme" for whatever the speaker (poet, politician, pundit, peasant—whatever) does to achieve this and what the dreamer involuntarily does ("poieseme": combining the Greek root already familiar to us through words like "poiesis" and the suffix used for familiar structural units such as "phoneme"). Let's look at six sets of poiesemes, that is, poetic strategies and devices. The set of six sets is fairly complete, but only illustrative subcategories can be mentioned below.

One kind of poieseme simply describes or presents sights, sounds, and the like. Such descriptions are always subject to symbolic interpretation. Such descriptions obviously include a gashed knee or a color such as blue-green and have been the fundamental idea in imagistic and objectivist poetics.

A second group consists of about six devices that shift emotions for aesthetic effect: the vocative mood, the shades of irony, sudden outrage at the slaughter of a bird—all illustrate the modal poiesemes that would, incidentally, be emphasized in an expressive or emotive theory of poetic language.

A third group is essentially formal in that it includes the addition, deletion, permutation, and internal ordering of dream atoms. While this is analogous to the syntax of a natural language, it is complicated by crossing over between types of perception and structure and by orders that may not be linear. A type of complex poieseme that may be particularly crucial in politically-concerned dreams flips all the values in the dream by virtue of one transformative symbol—often near the end.

A fourth set of poiesemes involves juxtaposition or contiguity in space, time, or some similar dimension; for example, a gang of young toughs may be juxtaposed to a painter in a yarmulke. These processes of metonym and anatomical relation are not coordinate with the metaphor and similar analogical poiesemes that, for example, connect cobblestoned streets, "Italianate squares," and corrugated bark.

Another, paired set of poiesemes involves expansion and contraction—most obviously in the release of gist that characterizes the "expanding ripples" of haiku and the riddlelike gist of skaldic and some Modernist poetry. Note that the gist of a dream or a poem is not a metaphor of it. What gist is alluded to by the word "Sharonne"?

A REINTERPRETATION OF "SHARONNE"

With the theoretical model just sketched and the provisional personal and public interpretations given above as contexts, let us return to the mysterious word "Sharonne." First note that it was pronounced with a strong gutteral trill, which could have been vaguely German or perhaps Israeli. Also that it slant rhymes with "heron" and so evokes the green and blue herons discussed earlier. But Sharon is also the name of the then Israeli defense minister, who was very much in the news as the organizer of the invasion of Lebanon, which he dubbed "Peace in Galilee"—peace, that is, for the long-suffering Jews threatened by forces identified by him with the Nazis and led by what he called another Hitler, Yasir Arafat. At this level I identify with the Jews: with my wife and her family and her Judaic studies, with the Jews of my passionately anti-Nazi German father, with my own Jewish great-grandfather Lazarus, with my long-standing affection for Hebrew, and with the Jewish souls who have inspired some of my published poems ("Chagall's Waltz," "Spinoza, I love you"). In sum, I am in part Jew.

There are different kinds of Jews but almost all see and represent Israel as the antithesis of Nazi Germany, which in many ways it is. And yet Sharon, a very self-righteous man, came to be held partly responsible for the much-publicized massacres at Shatila (i.e., Sha-plus Atila, or, for me, Attila the Hun, the German). Sharon was also heavily responsible for the less-publicized killing, maiming, and other suffering of thousands of Palestinian Arab women and children; as the most brilliant general in the Israeli army said in his resignation statement: "When I look through my binoculars, I see Arab children." Sharon was dubbed by some "The Butcher of Lebanon," and the invasion he led revealed militaristic, chauvinistic, racist, and genocidal aspects—which aroused widespread dissent and outrage in Israel. The dream shows that I am led to identify with the tragedy of the Palestinian Arabs, not so much in terms of their culture and the green banner of Islam, but because they—and most hauntingly their children—are human beings for whom one feels compassion.

And yet, to go further, it was Ariel Sharon who compounded the paradox of the Lebanese invasion with a statement—which I have used in another poem on so-called German war guilt—reminding us, the Americans, that we slaughtered vastly greater numbers of civilians of entire German cities in World War II. Specifically, I would add, over three million women and children were roasted, dismembered, and crushed to death in "that other holocaust," mainly as a consequence of saturation bombing attacks (mainly by the British) on densely populated residential areas. Despite my great ambivalence toward Germany, Germans, and German—I do not *particularly* like the German language, for example—I also identify with this cluster in terms of my anti-Nazi father and grandmother and other "good Germans," with German peasants, Catholics, and liberal-radicals, who were generally anti-Nazi, with the music of Bach and other "High Culture," and with the unpleasant fact that school situations have occasionally made me feel German—from protesting to my sixth-grade teacher that "the Germans did not start World War I" to intermittent encounters at the university level by persons who go too much by a last name. So I am part German, too.

My dream "Sharonne" condenses my identification with Jew, German, and, to a far lesser extent, Palestinian Arab and the severe conflicts resulting from these identifications, as well as such more abstract conflicts as high culture versus fascism, beauty versus obscenity, the brutality of war versus the sensitivies of peace. These and yet other conflicts are represented and condensed by the fact that the name of the militarist Sharon, leader of a so-called "Peace in Galilee" strike that was partly genocidal in intent, is also, for me at least, a name that connotes beauty and peace and love (e.g., "Rose of Sharon") in the Old Testament—a book containing many descriptions of genocidal warfare. The multiplex conflicts are brought to a point in the dream by what is its key act: the Jewish artist asks or begs me to judge his work, that is, him or implicitly Jews in general, and I, associated with Germans by blood, accept this role. The consequent guilt and shame is masked by a constructed, compensatory, idealized surface that, in this case, is identifiably neither German nor Jewish but cross-cultural or even anthropological. The dream claims that I am human in some sense that transcends ethnic and racist conflict.[2]

One sense in which this claim is made is that the poem (or I, a poet like Walt Whitman) exploits the entire repertoire of aesthetic strategies and devices that I call poiesemes: for example, phonic and visual images that startle; sudden shifts of mood (compassion, outrage); vivid juxtaposition of antithetical forms; metaphors and other analogies (e.g., between surfaces and projectile points); and, above all, the distillation of gist whereby ethnopolitical conflict is boiled down to a name. Curiously, "Sharonne" is governed, in part, by an overall chiasmus (see the outline in figure 4). To explicitly identify, label, and discuss each poieseme in "Sharonne" would take chapters. As a sort of shorthand I attach an inventory of poiesemes and an indication of some of those—such as the "constructional" chiasmus— that occur in the dream (table 5). One consequence of this aesthetic integration, even if it leaves the dreamer in a "troubled state," is

Figure 4. *Chiasmus*

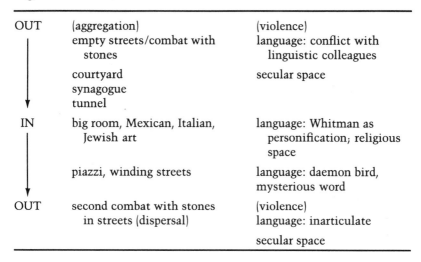

OUT	(aggregation) empty streets/combat with stones	(violence) language: conflict with linguistic colleagues
	courtyard synagogue tunnel	secular space
IN	big room, Mexican, Italian, Jewish art	language: Whitman as personification; religious space
	piazzi, winding streets	language: daemon bird, mysterious word
OUT	second combat with stones in streets (dispersal)	(violence) language: inarticulate
		secular space

a sense of healing or at least a sense of therapy, of "having been washed." The "master down there" has done his work.

Even from this brief summary it is clear that the dreamer—with half a dozen groups of poiesemes, each of them with a half dozen or more subtypes—has at his/her disposal an extremely complex means for generating the many-chambered reality of a dream.[3] My theoretical contention (already dealt with above) is that metaphor in both dream/dream interpretation and poetry/poetics has been overemphasized and also confused with analogy in a rhetorical or naive way. Metaphor in the familiar sense of a trope with a vehicle and a tenor is, of course, found in all speakers and dreamers; everybody is part poet. But the overemphasis on the metaphor in dream interpretations (e.g., Freud) reflects a perduring rationalism in Western thought, a sort of intellectual and methodological ethnocentrism.

CONCLUSION

So much has been written on the interpretation of dreams that—as with the Navajo or Homer—some would seriously question that anything new can be said about it. Granted that *nothing* is totally new, I would also point out that the interpretation of dreams in this century has been heavily biased in a few privileged directions, each

Table 5. *Dream Poiesemes*

Descriptive Poiesemes	
definition	
image	"young toughs are cruising"
lists	
narrative	
Modal Poiesemes	
outrage	
irony-sarcasm	"weeping with outrage"
doubt-skepticism	
Formal Poiesemes	
parallelism	
chiasmus	"quartz cuts my kneecap/
syntactic	I peg rock after rock"
Contiguity Poiesemes	
deixis	
apostrophe	"the green of earth"
metonym	
Analogical Poiesemes	
icon	
similarity	"cobblestoned streets : : corrugated bark"
metaphor	
Condensation/Expansion	
climax/closure	
gist	
proverb	"Sharonne"
expansion	

of them implying a few favored assumptions. Well over 90 percent of dream interpretation clusters around the following concerns or orientations: derivation of the dream from infancy or at least early childhood (e.g., my brother and I marching through Paris—in German toy war gear!); derivation from sexual and similar biological needs, satisfactions, fantasies, and so forth; derivation from literary, depth-psychological, or anthropological-mythic archetypes of various sorts, whether universal or cultural (e.g., the Russian model of the poet-as-fighter); derivation from immediate physical (e.g., somatic) stimuli preceding or during the dream (e.g., an encounter with a gang of adolescent Blacks on the streets of Hyde Park). Other dream interpretations have a practical or pragmatic focus, be it the spirit medium or the psychiatrist, with their concerns to predict, prognosticate, and heal.

Naturally, the number of arguably political dreams is going to vary by individual and culture; and it would be fallacious to reduce or derive clearly apolitical dreams from sources in the power matrix. Within the broad spectrum of contents and structures that one would want to call "political," some of the most intense involve racial and/or ethnic relations and identity. In large part this intensity stems from the symbolic interconnections between family, tribe, ethnic group, and nation; the envy-jealousy of family and kinship gets projected onto the tribal/ethnic/national screen. What I have been calling "the poetry of language" is no more intense in political than in apolitical dreams, but it is also no *less* intense, and, since it helps the dream to do its job of converting a conflict into a work of art—all dreams are works of art—and idealizing those conflicts, an understanding of this poetry is indispensable to discovering and unraveling the political gist.

This analysis of dreams from a politically centered or focused point of view leads, as in the foregoing example, to a creative integration of anthropology, poetics, political science, and the various psychologies, to an understanding of what I have called "the master down there" or what Homer called "the message from God" ("dreams come from God"). It might be objected that an antireductionist model such as I have proposed, which keeps homing in on the political—relating the political dream, the political gist, and the external politics of the dreamer and the dreamer's world—would mark a return to Homer and the Bible. This is true in that Homer and the Bible focus on political dreams and largely ignore all others; from a Homeric and biblical point of view, dream interpretation should be a subfield of the art of government, and of the discipline of political science. On the other hand, the theory of "the language of poetry in the politics of dreams," with its system of oneiremes and poiesemes—both as interpretive tools—is conceptually very different and more self-conscious than the remarkable insights provided by archaic seers that we still find so suggestive. Dream interpretation is the richer for integrating primitive modes of thought with those of the contemporary sciences and humanities—granted the de facto pluralism of theory today and the inevitably great indeterminacy in the interpretation of dreams, where "God's truth" cannot be known.

My conclusion—and suggestion for the future—is that a dream such as the above and a large fraction of other dreams are fundamentally political. They are *about* ethnic and racial conflicts, war, the vendetta, threats of fascism, and so forth. These and similar types of conflict may be contextualized in the here-and-now of a neighbor-

hood, party, nation, even a family—whatever. But it is the underlying relations of power that organize and drive the dreams. Another
indication of this power base is the way that, turning the tables,
dreams can become the input to politics: as the basis for motivation
in leaders, as the source of slogans and other condensed symbols, or
as part of political speeches in many cultures. For the interpreter of
such dreams—of dreams in politics and of politics in dreams—to go
back to infant experiences, sexual fantasies, mythic-universal archetypes, perceptual clues, and the like *does* yield much insight, but it
may be a collateral insight and should not lead us to avoid the political gist of many dreams and their relation to political problems in
the world.[4]

As a sort of epilogue, one consequence of analyzing "Sharonne"
and then writing up the results and discussing them with various
persons was that, one morning, I was able to recast the text into
what is formally a poem:

"Sharonne"

Streets Deserted. Gangs of Hard Youth.
Aviator Jackets. Cruising, They Pelt
Each Other with Quartz. I Quit. Insults.
My Right Kneecap Is Cut.

I turn into the corridor of a synagogue
through tunnel corridors until the major room
all hung about with paintings—orange, green, on white.
A youthful artist in a yarmulke. He begs
me: "Judge them!" I do and saunter out again
like Whitman in his floppy hat and on into
Italianate, paved squares, uneven, winding walks
with sycamores and telephone poles aslant,
the hooligans watching from an alley as

                    a green heron
                    greener than earth
                    greener than green
                    than the chartreuse-
                    turquoise color
                    I call "Sharonne"
                    starts up from a

different kind
of hardwood to
perch on a wire.

A hooligan's stone
cracks its wing.

It flits up, swerves back to the
corrugated bark of a locust tree
to cling and claw and drops straight down to me.
It tips its head. It flaps piteously.
I peg rock and rock after rock, screaming
in all directions down and off those streets.

As a contrast with the epilogue, there follows a second poem in the language of dreams—without politics.

First Draft

out of the rock of night I am herding three elephants
through a narrow pass that nearly swallows us and down wide
barren wasteland mountainsides ringed by massive walls of red
    brick
with the portals we are trooping through as a cosmic storm
    breaks—
icy rain sleeting, the lightning's Sanskrit hieroglyphs in shreds as I
    start
the little wrinkled fellows up the opposite slope and see suddenly
one wants to calve—I worry and the other two wait around
anxiously, but the rain is abating, and she calves without trouble
the petite trunk and the stuck-down ears sliding slimy out from
    between
the distended labia onto the frosted grass—it is a she-elephant the
    mother
licks clean and eats the brown afterbirth and the calf wobbling like
    stilts
we resume our ascent. The sky at dawn is clearing over this part of
    India:
mountain air the purity of oxygen, and a far away white-on-blue

6

The Unheralded Revolution in the Sonnet: Toward a Generative Model

There is a sort of continuum from a routine conversation to stylized and deeply conventional poetic forms such as the sestina and the sonnet. The sonnet illustrates one extreme case of "poetic language," with acutely constraining rules, patterns, and conventions of all sorts for all levels of sound and meaning. The sonnet, in its gradual changes through history, could serve as an (ideologically conservative) model for a disquisition on "poetry as a cultural system" or as a fascinating instance of a poetic form limited to and deeply ingrained in a linguistically demarcated area (European languages, plus Bengali).[1] It could also be made to serve an argument for extreme limitations on the individual imagination and hence as a qualification to some of the arguments in this book.

But the language of the sonnet—almost as a converse to the language of dreams—can illustrate the fissures and even the breakdown of order and convention in several ways. Beneath even the apparently rigid paradigms of the Petrarchan sonnet we find a set of formal principles that actually allow for unexpected freedoms of choice and mode—freedoms refreshingly realized by formative sonneteers such as Petrarch himself and Thomas Wyatt. In historical terms again, the premises and potential of the sonnet have recently been loosened up—sometimes exploded—so that today the scope of poetic indeterminacy in the sonnet outweighs the limitations of form; the sonnet actually can open into realms of chaos and indeterminacy while at the same time the individual poems are ordered in diversified and often novel ways. Like dreams, the sonnet form has become a multi-visionary means for perceiving and constructing order amid chaos, but also, unlike dreams, of giving intimations of the chaos beneath order and even within order.

THE SONNET IN AMERICA TODAY (1)

To American readers of poetry today as well as to the great majority of our poets the sonnet, like the minuet, is well defined—and passé. Our immediate associations are with Shakespeare, then with Keats and other Romantics (including recent ones such as Millay), and then with the Italian Renaissance. When pressed, the more informed will stipulate fourteen lines in iambic pentameter. And some will recall two structures: the Shakespearean, with three quatrains and a couplet, and the Petrarchan, with an octave followed by a sestet. Sophisticates will remember expanded and contracted sonnets, perhaps unrhymed sonnets, and so forth. And, depending on the universe of discourse, there are semantic notions about stepped progression, logical turns, an argument (thesis, development, resolution), and commitment to "one idea." But the structure of the sonnet, like that of the sonata, is not widely known or discussed.

In our thousands of creative writing classes the sonnet is, like haiku, assigned for a couple of weeks of edifying exercises and basic poetic literacy. But the overwhelming fact of our poetic consciousness is that the sonnet is known, taught, and written as a limited, traditional, conventional, rigid form. A magazine that publishes many sonnets, such as *Plains Poetry Journal*, is unusual. But even in such journals the enormous variation and play that the most traditional rules allow is generally ignored by contributors and editors alike, and the sonnets that appear are almost invariably strictly Shakespearean or Petrarchan. Likewise ignored is the wholesale revolution in the sonnet form that, granted a few pioneers (John Clare, Alexander Pushkin), has largely been achieved by poets such as Frost and Mallarmé writing since the latter part of the last century. Let us turn to two interrelated problems: the obvious freedom of the new practices and the underlying or implicit freedoms in the old rules. We begin with a general, historical background but, after the arrival of the sonnet in England, focus on the English and then the American tradition.

CULTURAL-HISTORICAL SKETCH OF THE FORM

The sonnet ("little sound/song") is one of those rarities in culture history: a complex artifact invented only once by someone whose identity is certain. Giacomo da Lentino (fl. 1215–33), one of the Sicilians among the poets surrounding the poet-king Frederick II, invented the sonnet. Fourteen lines of eleven syllables each were structured as two quatrains devoted to exposition and development (*abababab*) and a double refrain of two tercets devoted to the resolution (usually *cdecde*, with *cdcdcd* read as two tercets). The structure itself invited a sharp break or "turn" after the octave. Although the Frederician group was in close touch with Provençal and the German Minnesingers, the sonnet derives from Sicilian (and Arabic) folk song.

This economical and condensed form caught on, became high fashion, and was practiced and refined by other thirteenth-century Sicilians, notably Guido d'Arezzo, who introduced the octave *abba-abba*. Soon afterward poets on the Italian mainland, outstandingly, of course, Dante (1265–1321) and Petrarch (1304–74), gave the form great authority, made the line more flexible, and added several kinds of concluding sestet, particularly the relatively asymmetrical *cde-dce*. Many other variants appeared, notably the "tailed" (lengthened) sonnet, the tetrameter sonnet, the retrograde sonnet (with palindrome rhyme), and of course the terza rima sonnet (which violates the strong Italian constraint against a final couplet). The sonnet, with its Classical, Italian, and Catholic symbolism, evolved into a sort of national art form that was used for many themes, addresses, and purposes, including political ones: the morning after a political happening in Florence, dozens of sonnets would appear on the walls. And it was practiced by persons of high and low degree; Michelangelo, for example, is held by some authorities to be an important sonneteer. The Italian sonnet is exemplified by the poem "Tears" by Lizette Woodward Reese (1865–1935) (here and elsewhere I shall try to bring the sonnet into the present by using twentieth-century examples).

Tears

When I consider Life and its few years—
A wisp of fog betwixt us and the sun;
A call to battle, and the battle done
Ere the last echo dies within our ears;
A rose choked in the grass; an hour of fears;
The gusts that past a darkening shore do beat;
The burst of music down an unlistening street—
I wonder at the idleness of tears.
Ye old, old dead, and ye of yesternight,
Chieftains, and bards, and keepers of the sheep,
By every cup of sorrow that you had,
Loose me from tears, and make me see aright
How each hath back what once he stayed to weep;
Homer his sight, David his little lad!

Reese's rhyme scheme illustrates the kind of creative variation to be explored below: rather than having a regular octave, she shifts to c (*abbaacca*, which is slant rhymed with the first and fourth lines of the sestet. Her thematic structure, on the other hand, is conventional).

At the center of the medieval Jewish world, Italian Jews such as Immanuel of Rome were writing canonical Italian sonnets in the thirteenth century, albeit in Arabic quantitative meter; but this speech community soon shifted to other directions.

After the sonnet acquired the Italian imprimatur that it still retains, it diffused into other parts of what was to become the sonnet world. It "took" in Provence only somewhat later than on the Italian mainland, and inspired many of the leading troubadors. It arrived on the Iberian Peninsula in the early fifteenth century, was established and produced prolifically by Lope de Vega and others during the "Century of Gold," and has been a basic tradition of Portuguese and Spanish literature ever since (particularly in Mexico). In northern France it had, by the sixteenth century, become a primary form for Ronsard (1524–85) and his circle, and it has attracted many of France's greatest poets, notably Baudelaire, Mallarmé, and Valéry (all using the hexameter). The strength of the sonnet in France and of the French tradition among us is illustrated by Yeats's version of the Ronsard classic: "When you are old and grey and full of sleep, / And nodding by the fire, take down this book, / And slowly read, and dream of the soft look / Your eyes had once, and of their shadows deep. . . ."

Elsewhere we find the sonnet spreading more slowly into the Germanies, not actually reaching them until the seventeenth century, and practiced in a relatively intermittent and uneven way in subsequent years: Rilke is probably the high point in the Germanic community and the greatest influence on sonnet writing in the United States today. The sonnet has been a major form in Greece, forming a sort of companion to the Italian sonnet, and it has been important in Yugoslavia for similar reasons. But in general the sonnet reached the Slavs very late—four to six centuries after Dante—and, for cultural reasons, has played a far lesser role in their literatures. Yet it was used at some point by most of the major Russian poets, such as Mandelstam; and Alexander Pushkin, for his major work, *Eugene Onegin,* "a novel in verse," devised a totally new variant (to which I return below).

Before considering the English-speaking peoples, let me make three general points. The first, which I can barely document, is that thousands of unknown and even unpublished poets have been inspired to write dozens or even hundreds of sonnets; once in a while a great one such as "Tears" is rescued from oblivion. Second, not only are most major sonneteers also major poets, but many of the greatest poets have been drawn to the sonnet. What has attracted them has been significantly independent of cognitive, philosophical, and other considerations at the level of meaning. The content of their sonnets has, in fact, ranged from the courtly eros of Plutarch to Rilke's metaphysics of vision to Baudelaire's often concrete visions of evil to Pushkin's energized narratives and utterly colloquial conversations; perhaps the most basic dimensions amid this variation have been (1) the courtly-elegant versus the colloquial style and (2) profane versus sacred subject matter. But what has fascinated these and other poets and often inspired their poems have been problems of the form of the sonnet.

THE SONNET IN ENGLISH

The sonnet was introduced to England by Thomas Wyatt (1503–42), who, while writing mainly in the variants that he had learned as a diplomat in Italy, also innovated in the *way* he broke the sestet into a quatrain plus a couplet: *cdcdee.* This is the frame for what in my judgment perdures as the most brilliant and forceful sonnet in the English language: [2]

> Whoso list to hunt, I know where is an hind,
>   But as for me, *hélas*! I may no more.
>   The vain travail hath wearied me so sore,
> I am of them that furthest come behind.
> Yet may I, by no means, my wearied mind
>   Draw from the deer; but as she fleeth afore
>   Fainting I follow. I leave off therefore,
> Since in a net I seek to hold the wind.
> Who list her hunt, I put him out of doubt,
>   As well as I may spend his time in vain;
>   And graven with diamonds in letters plain
> There is written, her fair neck round about,
>   "Noli me tangere, for Caesar's I am,
>   And wild for to hold, though I seem tame."

Wyatt's innovations were completed by his near contemporary, Henry Howard, Earl of Surrey, to yield a sonnet with three distinct quatrains (*ababcdcdefef*) and a concluding couplet (*gg*), hence a maximization of rhyme, a relatively stepped progression, and a strong sense of closure. After Surrey, Spenser (1552–99) invented a melodic, concatenated variant (*ababbcdccdcee*) that, despite its great potential, has been used but rarely since. Then Surrey's scheme was given "deathless" prestige by Shakespeare's 154 sonnets.

It is the Italian forms, however, that have been somewhat favored—for example, by Donne (1573–1631) and Milton (1608–74), the latter of these revolutionizing the sonnet by dropping the sharp break midway and giving the whole poem a single, continuous vision; both took the sonnet away from song and toward a more conceptual focus. Granted some partial exceptions such as Cowper, it can be said that the sonnet was eclipsed by the Neoclassical forms of the late seventeenth and the eighteenth centuries—as it was in Europe generally. But it reemerged as one of the essential vehicles for the Romantic movement, favored and developed by Keats, Shelley, Wordsworth (who wrote over five hundred sonnets), E. B. Browning, Longfellow, and later by the Rossettis and many others. In general, the Italian and the Shakespearean variants were adhered to rather rigidly.

SUMMARY: SURFACE STRUCTURE

Except in the hands of isolated geniuses, the sonnet, until Hopkins and the French Modernists, was governed overwhelmingly by certain rules, most of which, in the conventional view that prevails, are still observed today (some of these are not, of course, peculiar to the sonnet).

The Line. A metrically regular (usually iambic pentameter) line, either with a strong caesura or with a marked increase or thrust of energy in the center. The line, in either case, is strongly felt as a unit, and enjambment is highly marked.

Rhyme. The rule is regular, full rhymes, including many in the same part of speech and even the same inflectional form. The indispensable end rhyme is balanced by internal texture in various ways (alliteration in English, internal rhyme). Overall schemes are of the Italian or English varieties already discussed.

Vision and/or Logical Structure. The sonnet usually argues a single idea, with a break near the middle (accompanied by a full stop between the octave and sestet) or with an argument in three parts— or both (in the sense that there are two interacting structures). As a continuing feature, the sonnet is, at the same time, both markedly stichic and markedly strophic.

Variation. These surface rules lead to many natural variations. Starting with an *abab* sequence, the second quatraine can be reversed, as in Sidney, to *baba;* or an initial octave in *abab* or *abba* can be followed by *cdcd.* On the other hand, an overall chiasmic structure (e.g., *abbaabbaabba*) creates a quite different phonic potential. A different, recursive potential can be achieved by looping back to *ab* in the sestet or the couplet (as in Josephine Miles's "Tally"). Many other variations were devised in the Renaissance or since or have been infused with new life, as in Frost's "Acquainted with the Night," which includes twelve lines in terza rima, then a concluding couplet.

THE MODERN PERIOD

The Modernist—or, perhaps better, the modern period between the late nineteenth and mid-twentieth centuries—witnessed a curious bifurcation. On the one hand, four "giants" of those years eschewed the sonnet because, for example, it was associated too much with traditional forms such as the iambic pentameter, or tended to entail the completion of a rhyme scheme with padded lines, or was too dependent on a Renaissance-style "argument." Eliot, Moore, Stevens, and Williams wrote practically no sonnets (Williams opposed them explicitly), and this despite the fact that all four participated significantly in the American version of the Romantic tradition and were close students of the Renaissance lyric and of modern literature in the Romance languages (or at least of French in the case of Moore and Stevens). To some extent, they wanted to perpetuate not the form but some of the spirit or world view traditionally associated with and expressed through the sonnet. Yeats, Pound, and Auden seem intermediate: they crafted some superb sonnets but contributed little to its evolution. Some lesser poets added great sonnets to the tradition: Crane, Jeffers, Millay, Robinson, and Owen. Four other "giants" of Modernism, on the other hand, practiced and even favored the sonnet and innovated radically: Hopkins in line length, sprung rhythm, and overall phonic texture; Frost in line rhythms and rhyme schemes; Lawrence in diction and dialect; Cummings in intonation and stanzaic structure. And all four of these poets moved the sonnet closer to conversation.

The troubled, liminal period between the poets just mentioned and the self-conscious pluralism of today went in two directions. Half or so of the leading poets, including Bishop, Jarrell, Roethke, and Olson, ignored the sonnet because of its cultural associations or because its formal powers lead in directions quite different from the ones they were seeking. But many southern poets such as Tate and Ransom did write many sonnets, as did Lowell, Berryman, and their sympathizers, partly in reaction to the Modernists, partly to explore new possibilities such as the unrhymed sonnet; in *History*, Lowell eventually generated 568 "pseudo-sonnets," which, whatever one may think about their quality, opened up a loose and accessible variant of the form to many younger poets.

MORE SURFACE VARIATION

Given the considerable surface constraints just noted as well as others, we find a number of innovations that we can group in terms of initial units of various kinds, two-part divisions, cutting and extending the sonnet, and deviating from the isometric (usually pentameter) line.

Against one powerful rule, which precludes an initial couplet, we find Frost's "The Oven Bird" ("There is a singer everyone has heard / Loud, a mid-summer and a mid-wood bird"). And against an equally powerful constraint, which precludes starting with a sestet, we find his "Mowing" (see below; there is at least one precedent for this, Shelley's "England in 1819").

There are other variations. Herrick's "I sing of brooks," Clare's "Evening Primrose," and Frost's "Once by the Pacific" are all in seven couplets. We occasionally find a sonnet consisting of the seven-line stanzas—for instance, in Robinson's "The Companion." These symmetrical sonnets break the strong rule of dynamic asymmetry in overall form (which is reminiscent of the rule against a sixth-foot caesura in the dactylic hexameter line).

The extended or "tailed" sonnet of the Renaissance reappears, and Hopkins invents the curtailed sonnet, notably exemplified in "Pied Beauty." Semisonnets (four united quatrains) had been devised by George Meredith (1828–1909), as in his "Modern Love," and other semisonnets have followed since then. To this I would add the "intended sonnet," where what by various criteria was meant to be a sonnet and still feels like one has veered away from the norms of line length, number of lines, and so forth, conventional rules being sacrificed to what the poem is trying to be: for example, Owen's magnificent war poem "Futility." On the dimension of line length, short-liners of many kinds have appeared or reappeared, a typical case being Wylie's Italian "little sonnet" in iambic tetrameter. Much less orthodox have been the experiments of Kinnell and Ashbery; the latter's "Dido" begins, "The body's products become / Fatal to it. Our spit / Would kill us, but we / Die of our heat." Long-line sonnets were pioneered by Hopkins; "The Windhover," for instance, runs to seventeen-syllable lines that break the limits of the printer's page, to wit: ". . . king- / dom of daylight's dauphin, dapple-dawn-drawn Falcon, in his riding." No one has tried to combine a Whitman-style long line with the sonnet format, but this has potential and would technically syncretize two traditions that have long been basic in American poetry. Other, actually realized variations involve the interaction of a real or implied rhyme scheme with forms on the printed page that are unconventional; for example, Cummings's unrhymed sonnet "you shall in all things be glad and young" has the lines grouped in the following blocks on the page: 2-4-2-4-2. These questions of visual layout and other so-called concrete effects of the printed page are maximally removed from the sonnet-as-song values of the Renaissance, or, later, the concern with the potential music of language among sonneteers such as the Rossettis.

GENERATIVE RULES

As has been known for centuries, the octave invented by Guido d'Arezzo can be read at least three ways: as three couplets bracketed by a rhyme, as two quatrains, and as two quatrains overlapping with a quatrain (or even two tercets bracketing a couplet). This can be diagrammed as follows:

a (*bb aa bb*) *a*
abba   abba
ab(*ba   ab*)*ba*
abb (*aa*) bba

The sestet, too, can be read variously, which means that the sonnet as a whole is always phonically ambiguous to a high degree, or, in other words, that several levels of rhyme have to work together more or less simultaneously. By the same logic, the sonnet should not be conceptualized in terms of overt rhyme schemes but in terms of combinatory possibilities that can be generated by a set of underlying givens.

Three things normally are assumed for the octave: symmetry, the minimum of two rhymes, and no initial couplet. This leaves the following possibilities:

I	II	
abba	*abba*	
abab	*abab*	= 6 octaves
	aabb	

of which the two with *aabb* in position II would be marginal.

If we then assume up to three rhyme words in the tercet (*c, d, e*), we get the following sestets: *cdecde, cedced,* and so forth. Of the mathematically possible sestets, Petrarch favored at least four: couplets (*cdcdcd*), repeated, symmetrical tercets (particularly *cdecde* and *cdccdc*), and asymmetrical tercets (particularly *cdedce*). Even within these limits there are four times four or sixteen totally conventional Italian sonnet forms. But at least one anthologized English-language sonnet in the Italian style has been found that ends in one out of fifteen of the total number of possible sestets. If we multiply this total of fifteen sestets times the total of four (non-

Figure 5. The Sestets (following an octave in *a* and *b* only)

Italian #1	*c*	*d*	*e*	*c*	*d*	*e*	Berryman, "Sonnet 25"
Italian #2	*c*	*d*	*c*	*d*	*c*	*d*	Hopkins, "Carrion Comfort"
Italian #3	*c*	*d*	*e*	*d*	*c*	*e*	Cummings, "Next to of course God—America I"
	c	*d*	*e*	*e*	*d*	*c*	Auden, "Who's Who"
	c	*d*	*c*	*e*	*d*	*e*	Auden, "Our Bias"
cd-	*c*	*d*	*e*	*c*	*e*	*d*	Wordsworth, "On the beach at Calais"
	c	*d*	*d*	*e*	*c*	*e*	Thomas, "February Afternoon"
	c	*d*	*c*	*e*	*e*	*d*	Robinson, "Souvenir"
	c	*d*	*d*	*c*	*e*	*e*	Pushkin, *Eugene Onegin* (Nabokov)
	c	*d*	*c*	*d*	*e*	*e*	Frost, "Putting in the Seed"
	c	*c*	*d*	*e*	*e*	*d*	Frost, "Range-Finding"
cc-	*c*	*c*	*d*	*d*	*e*	*e*	Berryman, "The Poet's Final Instructions"
	c	*c*	*d*	*e*	*d*	*e*	Robinson, "How Annandale Went Out"
II c-d	*c*	*d*	*c*	*c*	*d*	*c*	Frost, "Design"
	c	*d*	*d*	*c*	*d*	*c*	Santayana, "O World"
	c	*d*	*d*	*c*	*c*	*d*	?
	c	*c*	*d*	*c*	*c*	*d*	Hopkins, "I Wake and Feel the Fell of Dark"
III	*c*	*c*	*c*	*c*	*c*	*c*	?

marginal) octaves, we get a total of sixty possible rhyme schemes with a good precedent in our language. The sestets that I have found, with the names of the poets and the poems, are tabulated below in figure 5.

SUGGESTIVE CONSTRAINTS

The enormous formal potential of even the conventional sonnet is constrained in the most diverse ways.

Sonnets—even a sestet—in triplets are precluded; in English, at least, this is simply an intensification of the limitations and difficulties inherent in the triplet. Given the incantatory power of triplets, a triplet sonnet remains a possibility.

A number of other sestets are not used in English, or at least are very rare: *effgge* (in Auden's "Who's Who") and *cddcdd* and *cdedce* (which are common in Italian—Petrarch also has *cdcece* [in XXVI] and even, with a triplet, *cdddcc* [XIII]).

The sonnet with a retracted, that is, nonfinal couplet, is rare, although the *ccdeed* variant was used by Dante Gabriel Rosetti, who was, of course, exceptionally close to the Italian tradition. The *ccdede* variant occurs once in my sample ("How Annandale Went Out"), but the fact that even in French it had to be championed by F. de Malherbe (1555–1629) in a swirl of poetics controversy suggests that powerful constraints are at work. Incidentally, Pushkin used this sestet in one of his rare sonnets, "Madonna."

It was Pushkin, too, who invented a form of the sonnet that occurs in the work of no other poet in no other language except in the imitative work of Nabokov and similarly derivative writing. Yet this scheme would be singularly appropriate for English because it maximizes not only the number of (perfect) rhymes but the possible overall variation (assuming multiples of two) as follows: *abab ccdd effe gg*. Consider the following superb translation by Arndt of *Eugene Onegin* 5.2:

> Winter . . . the peasant, feeling restive,
> Breaks a new trail with sledge and horse;
> Sensing the snow, his nag is restive
> And manages a trot of sorts;
> Here passes, powdery furrows tracing,
> A spirited kibítka, racing,
> The coachman on his box a flash
> Of sheepskin coat and crimson sash.
> There runs a yard-boy, having chosen
> To seat his "Rover" on the sled,
> Himself hitched up in horse's stead;
> The rascal rubs one finger, frozen
> Already, with a wince and grin,
> While Mother shakes her fist within.

The constraints enumerated above suggest that the sonnet is often controlled by formal and cultural factors that are relatively subtle and remain to be explored. For one thing, the greater formal variation among the Italians (and persons imbued with Italian such as Pushkin and D. G. Rossetti) suggests that the "native" imagines *il sonneto* more in the generative terms that I have outlined, whereas, except for master experimentalists such as Frost and Robinson, the English-speaking poet thinks of the Italian sonnet in terms of a memorized surface rhyme scheme.

BREAKING THE RULES

In the twentieth century so many variations on the sonnet have emerged that we are in a new sonnet world. These innovations have involved the (unmetered) line, rhyme (e.g., unrhymed versus full rhyme), the role of enjambment, overall gestalt, the continuity of meaning, the types of subject matter, and the attitudes and stance of the poet. Consonant with my general contention that the gist and appeal of the sonnet is primarily formal, let us look at some of the variation in the limited area emphasized in this article: the overall rhyme scheme seen, not as random or incidental variation, but as poets' strategies that arguably contribute to the power of the sonnet.

In one kind of innovation the poet adheres to a conventional format except for one obvious break. Thus, John Crowe Ransom (1888–1974) ends his Shakespearean "Winter Remembered" with "And there I went, the hugest winter blast / Would have this body bowed, these eyeballs streaming"—where "blast" does not rhyme with earlier lines in the poem, and "streaming" only slant rhymes with "-ealing" in lines ten and twelve.

In a second kind, intensification is achieved through cumulative slant rhyme, as in Laura Riding's "The Map of Places," which starts out $abb_1b_2b_3b_3b_4$ ("passes . . . tears . . . are . . . were . . . her . . . there"), and then concludes with four couplets. Hart Crane's sonnet to Emily Dickinson, in a diametrically opposite order, starts with four couplets—which also can be read as two quatrains—and then shifts to ddd_1d_1 before the final couplet *ee*. Clearly, the repetitiveness of several perfectly rhymed couplets is being played against the freshness of rhymes that are not only slanted but cumulatively so.

By a third general strategy, an overall symmetry of rhyme is preserved even while departing from the traditional formats. Merrill Moore (1903–57), in more than one thousand published sonnets, provides some of the most interesting and numerous innovations in this direction—for example, a rhyme scheme that can be bracketed as follows: *abc deed ff bac ff.* Moore's sonnets hit upon a significant fraction of the mathematically possible full-rhyme schemes.

Fourth, an expectation of rhyme may be created by the initial lines but then be frustrated in various ways. A poem can start with *abba* in iambic pentameter tone and then veer off in the direction of open form. Hopkins, on the other hand, begins "The Windhover" with an octave in final "-ing" before shifting to a regular sestet. In his phonically extraordinary "When I read Shakespeare—" Lawrence shifts asymmetrically between several full and slant rhymes: "wonder . . . thunder . . . *language* . . . daughters . . . rougher . . . chuffer . . . *with* . . . snoring . . . whoring . . . choring . . . goring . . . daggers . . . are . . . gas-tar." Mandelstam uses only *a* and *b* in his poem "Pedestrian": *abab baba bab aba.* Mallarmé's equally brilliant "The Virgin, The Vivid, and the Splendid New Day" revels in final assonance: "aujourd'hui . . . ivre . . . givre . . . fui . . . liu . . . livre . . . vivre . . . ennui . . . agonie . . . nie . . . pris . . . assigne . . . mépris . . . Cygne" (where octave and sestet are clearly indicated, however).

Some of the most interesting sonnets display unordered or at least highly asymmetrical variation. Kinnell in his "In Fields of Summer" shifts from *a* to *h* but then cuts back to $gg_1 ii_1 h$ ("look . . . flakes . . . deepening . . . up . . . dew"). Other modern sonnets verge on being prose spread over fourteen isometric lines, which may or may not be isometric. But let us close with Frost's "Mowing" because it illustrates the freshness and power of the move toward asymmetry. Using capital letters for the second member of a slant rhymed pair, we get:

ab c ab de c dE eD eD

which reflects several underlying groupings. On phonic grounds as well as in virtue of its many interacting meanings, Frost was justified in regarding "Mowing" as one of his best ("I come so near what I long to get that I almost despair of coming nearer"; Frost 1964: 83).

There was never a sound beside the wood but one,
And that was my long scythe whispering to the ground.
What was it it whispered? I knew not well myself;
Perhaps it was something about the heat of the sun,
Something, perhaps, about the lack of sound—
And that was why it whispered and did not speak.
It was no dream of the gift of idle hours,
Or easy gold at the hand of fay or elf:

Anything more than the truth would have seemed too weak
To the earnest love that laid the swale in rows,
Not without feeble-pointed spikes of flowers
(Pale orchises), and scared a bright green snake.
The fact is the sweetest dream that labor knows.
My long scythe whispered and left the hay to make.

Curiously, the sonnets that maximize overall variation of rhyme
to the point of lacking it and those that, on the contrary, minimize it
to the point of having only *one* end word, *both* eliminate the formal
(i.e., rhyme) counterpart to the bipartite semantic structure or argument that has usually been so integral to the sonnet tradition.

All poetry is experimental poetry.
    WALLACE STEVENS, *Opus Posthumous*

In symbolic studies today a major theoretical enterprise or exploration is to be explicit about subjective factors and to explicitly
relate one's authorial subjectivity to what used to be called the object of analysis. These explorations, depending on the author, may
derive from a Neo-Marxist epistemology or an Orientalist, existentialist, or phenomenological philosophy, or (as in my case) as an analogy from the principle of indeterminacy in physics ("the observer
is an integral part of the universe of observation"). Whatever the
sources—and they must be multiple in all cases—I subscribe to
these explorations and have already experimented many times, notably in *The Meaning of Aphrodite*; within the main focus of the
present chapter—"toward a generative model"—an essential constituent is my own experience and use of that model.

In the fall of 1982, having read thousands, memorized hundreds,
and written dozens over the years and having more time for writing
because of a Guggenheim, I decided to explore the inner form of the
sonnet while simultaneously writing a set myself. To use either of
the standard variants for my own work struck me as atavistic but
other options did not.

After some experimentation I resolved to more or less follow
certain guidelines.

There would be one central idea, but not necessarily an "argument."

I would use any of the rhyme schemes that could be generated by my model, but I would not sacrifice meaning or a good line simply to satisfy such a scheme. I would use slant rhyme, partly à la Dickinson, but often in the sense of "sounding alike" or being sufficiently similar in terms of the number of features shared by two forms in a close phonetic transcription (e.g., the "advent" and "gnats" rhyme in my poem below). Full rhyme was almost entirely for emphasis or other special effects. In other words, a complex system of potential rhyme would generate a poem, but the final surface form did not have to conform to one of the standard sonnet types in the "great tradition."

The lines would be isometric, with their length to be determined by the first line—my usual point of inspiration and departure when writing. These point-of-departure or jumping-off lines could range from nine to twelve syllables, or four to six stress or energy groups (my idea of "energy group" cannot be spelled out here). Despite isometricity, the length and semantic quality of the line should not, once again, be sacrificed by adding or deleting a canonical stress or syllable, more or less. At a more intuitive level, I would avoid a strong iambic pentameter or similar traditional sound or pattern. Thus line length was also part of a generative system rather than a procrustean surface.

Finally, there would be fourteen lines, with strong closure on the last two.

What was new about these guidelines was partly the combination: my particular use of slant rhyme in a sonnet and my definition of slant rhyme itself; the degree of variation not only allowable but allowable in terms of relatively explicit generative rules; and the idea of variable but generally isometric lines, whose length would be determined by the first line that had sprung into being. Other semantic criteria regarding metaphor and "keying," while also operative, will not be discussed here.

For over five months, for an hour or two each morning, early, I wrote sonnets, eventually completing about forty as well as redoing about twenty open or free-verse poems into sonnet form; a half dozen of my earlier poems *already were* sonnets by the new criteria. Typically, I would produce a complete draft in an hour or less on one day and then revise it over two or three days (often during long walks in downtown Chicago). My main experiences were: that these poems tended to fall into two parts simply as a consequence of mental energy—they tended to be composed in two bursts; that few readers noticed that I was using slant rhyme or, at readings, that they *were* sonnets; that stress groups and energy peaks yielded better lines, as a rule, than syllable counts; that some of my free-verse poems were improved by being put into sonnet form, whereas others were improved by being cast into sonnet and then *back* into various free or open forms.

As a sort of control and also to slow myself down I eventually began doing rough draft translations of all my sonnets into Russian. Attempts to have these translations finished by master translators (and native speakers) have indicated that on all counts, notably lexicon, the poems were highly untranslatable (which seems to imply, in the first instance, a relative embeddedness in the semantic nuances of American English).

Of the fifty-odd sonnets only sixteen, seven of them new (as opposed to those reworked from older poems), satisfied my criteria for quality. Of these, nine have been placed in professional poetry journals or in anthologies; one of the better of these (cited below) will appear in the *Kansas Quarterly* (1985). Although some of my sonnets were rewritten dozens of times over the months (scores or hundreds of times if we count "mental rewriting"), "Generation" remains a third draft.

Generation

The Hermit Thrush, crushed by tires in our alley
lies far from Guatemala, from the Yellow-Jacket
who hovers over the thrush's blood, expectantly.
Some message in the bird's code, genetic bits—
runes cut in a runestick—made it wing
south out of the White Pine stands of Ottawa
over the wheatfields like a man seeking home
or, perhaps more, a woman pressing inward
along the sidewalks of her mind that are cracked cement
with dead birds, but where witchgrass and plaintains
sprout in the fissures, pioneering the advent
of a weedy field, then bushes, and then again
high climax stands of conifers swarming with gnats
where thrushes will feed during the northern summer.

Having—to use trade lingo—included the participant-cum-observer in the universe of description, let us now return to that larger universe.

THE SONNET IN AMERICA TODAY (2)

Given the formal potential of even the conventional sonnet that was shown earlier, what is the status of the sonnet today? None of the fifty to one hundred established, recognized poets who have won or at least been nominated for major national prizes (so-called Mandarins) or, for that matter, who have been on the cover of *The American Poetry Review* currently write sonnets. Ashbery, Bly, Merrill, Merwin, Rich, and Snodgrass wrote sonnets long ago and some (notably Ashbery and Merrill) even published excellent sonnets, but they are not writing sonnets now or encouraging others to do so. The contemporary lack of enthusiasm for the sonnet increases among "pace-setting" younger poets such as Bidart, Dubie, Forché, Gallagher, Graham, Harrison, Strand, and Wakoski (granted, the last of these got started writing poetry with Shakespearean sonnets and has published a superb sestina). Among the poems by "poets under forty" (as of 1975), conscientiously selected for *The American Poetry Anthology*, not one sonnet appears. In fact, it is bizarre, even absurd, to think of the two groups of poets just named as advocating the sonnet. Apparently, recognized poets avoid the stigma of seeming to regress to the sonnet in an obvious way. Undeterred by these biases, however, let us look at some of the new possibilities as actually exemplified by recent poetry.

First we must ask: what is the sonnet today? Where, in American poetry, does one draw the line between the "canonical" sonnet and all other sonnetlike things? In my opinion only two sets of criteria survive. The first are specific and formal. Most poets and critics still hold to the skeleton of fourteen lines, even after everything else has been discredited. Somewhat less diagnostic is that the lines be of equal length, usually about the same visual length, and be reminiscent of iambic pentameter. Finally, there is the less obvious criterion that the rhymes and visual breaks between sections be in multiples of two, that is, that they involve division into equal sets; the only exceptions to this powerful criterion have been the innovations in the direction of randomness noted above. The second set of criteria is really a "fuzzy" set: some necessary and sufficient combination of diction, argument, world view, and perhaps a dozen other things (including, of course, line and rhyme). The basic answer to my initial question, however, is that *no* line exists nor should one be drawn between the many canonical sonnets and other sonnetlike and sonnetoid forms, including the grey marginal area of poems whose authors themselves would not want to call sonnets even though some of their meaning derives from vibrations and resonances within the sonnet world.

It is difficult to relate the conventional sonnet to today's poetic consciousness, notably its decentered pluralism. That the sonnet can still engage criticism is shown by Cunningham, Kelly, Liang, and a few other sonneteers. That sonnets can succeed with the general public is shown by the perennial sales of Millay in practically all major bookstores. Some well-known contemporaries, including Ashbery and Hollander, have written sets of sonnetlike lyrics predicated on a purely formal criterion or variation (e.g., thirteen lines, fifteen lines), with results that differ in spirit from the basically semantically motivated sonnets dealt with above. At the grass-roots level sonnets are produced in enormous quantities; for example, both the Poetry Club of Chicago and the Illinois State Poetry Society sponsor "international" competitions in both the Shakespearean and/or Petrarchan sonnet, and I am sure the same happens in some other states. A stronger argument for contemporary relevance is provided by the work of Claude McKay, as bitter, haunting, and "relevant" today as it was four decades ago during the "Harlem Renaissance."

The Harlem Dancer

Applauding youths laughed with young prostitutes
And watched her perfect, half-clothed body sway;
Her voice was like the sound of blended flutes
Blown by black players upon a picnic day.
She sang and danced on gracefully and calm,
The light gauze hanging loose about her form;
To me she seemed a proudly-swaying palm
Grown lovelier for passing through a storm.
Upon her swarthy neck black shiny curls
Luxuriant fell; and tossing coins in praise,
The wine-flushed, bold-eyed boys, and even the girls,
Devoured her shape with eager, passionate gaze;
But looking at her falsely-smiling face,
I knew her self was not in that strange place.

CONCLUSIONS AND SPECULATIONS

Even the limited area of rhyme dealt with in this article has demonstrated or suggested the potential of, for example, the phonic ambiguities of the octave, the many possible "multiples of two," the options of slant rhyme, and so forth. Once we leave the limits of rhyme and connect the sonnet with other formal dimensions such as the distribution of energy within the line, the total possibilities increase even more. The sonnet explodes when we enter various dimensions of semantics and emotions. Sonnets and sonnetlike poems can achieve a special poignancy or other psychological depth when they entail the realism and pessimism of Frost, the urbanity and idealism of Cummings, the urban neuroticism of Berryman, or the Black defiance and desperation of Claude McKay. The anguish, power, complexity, and occasional ugliness of these world views acquire a certain existential courage when they are ensconced in the implicitly measured, melodic; and generally Romantic forms of "the little song" invented seven centuries ago in Sicily by Giacomo da Lentino.

But this leaves unanswered the question with which I began: what is it about the *sound form* of the sonnet and sonnetlike poem that gives them such vitality and fascination? One answer lies in the arguments advanced by G. A. Miller in his famous article "The Magical Number Seven, Plus or Minus Two" (1957), where he showed that, both cognitively and perceptually, the mind tends to favor sets of about seven and tends to lose certain kinds of control as it goes above or below this number. The sonnet, with its phonic and semantic break about midway through fourteen lines, its lines of about five emphatic syllables and ten syllables in all, and other features of this sort, would seem to illustrate Miller's contention as much as the perceptual test data and lexical semantic data that he adduces. At all linguistic levels—phonetic, lexical, syntactic—the sonnet plays around the magical number.

In the second place, a fundamental fact about our linguistic consciousness is the rough dichotomy between the active and the passive command of a language—here sonnet language. While few poets today have an active command in this sense—shades of Florence in 1400!—practically all American poets and readers of poetry have read hundreds of sonnets and often include sonnets among the poems that they cherish and/or know by heart. That is why a poem that resonates within the sonnet world over time acquires a richness of meaning that few other forms can give. The gross historical fact is that the sonnet has been used, or better, achieved in many languages by a large fraction of the most enduring poets—Petrarch, Dante, Camões, Lope de Vega, Shakespeare, Milton, Keats, Baudelaire, Ronsard, Mallarmé, Pushkin, Mandelstam, Rilke, Goethe, Frost, Cummings, Vallejo. This alone would argue for its continued cumulative growth as a lyric form. As long as poets in the European languages study their craft seriously they will be studying a lot of sonnets, and poets such as McKay and Berryman will continue to arise. But the excellence of the poets and the persuasiveness of their poems do not account for the enduring appeal of the sonnet over seven centuries, any more than does "the magical number seven" and similar psychological, scientific arguments. Perhaps no other lyric form enables one to reach a sustained, energetic argument and/or vision *and* a strong sense of closure, of completion—in such short compass. But, after much consideration, the appeal of the sonnet remains, at least for me, something mysterious and largely unexplained.

7

The Poem as Parallactic Position: Seven Poems

Let us proceed along the routes established by the Tarascan poems in chapter 3 and the "Generation" poem in chapter 6. The seven poems that follow further illustrate the poetic shape of cultural patterning ("culture as a work of art"), even in a ritual as ordinary as most conversations and certainly in the culturally modelled encounter between the imagination of a poet and those of other persons in other cultures; cross-cultural encounters may be a sort of symbiosis headed toward convergence, or they may be cross-fertilization headed toward greater diversification. Finally, one of the poems relates poetic language to physiological and even metaphysical chaos. But let me introduce them more concretely.

The first poem, "Sketches for an Ode to 'The Yankee Clipper,'" is based on DiMaggio's *Lucky to be a Yankee* and Maury Allen's *Where Have You Gone, Joe DiMaggio?* The latter book, an exemplary piece of sports writing, drew on over 250 interviews with baseball folk of all sorts, from which I culled hundreds of sentences and phrases, eventually selecting and sorting them in an intuitively satisfying way—"intuitively satisfying" in the sense of capturing some of the public and archetypal meanings of "Joe D" but, more important, of juxtaposing and arranging these utterances so that their possible meanings would enhance and illuminate each other to give us what we hear in bars and ballparks all over this land. The verbal symbolism in the utterances is so densely entangled with cultural values, local meanings, and American and Latin values of honor and respect as to make the parts and the whole relatively impervious to translation—with the partial exception of analogical universes with similar baseball lingos and honor and shame complexes.

"I thought I saw some Eskimos" arises from the fusion of a mythic image with a linguistic, theoretical image. The latter, from Saussure, is that "language can also be compared with a sheet of paper: thought is the front and the sound the back; one cannot cut the front without cutting the back at the same time; likewise in language, one can neither divide sound from thought nor thought from sound" (1959:113). Language connects the universe of sound and the universe of meaning. In the immediately following Dakota poem, a half dozen or more personal, situational, and cultural contexts combine to intensify the meaning of a near-minimal bit of speech (Saussure's *parole*).

"Where does it end" seeks to impart the phonic, that is, the perceptual, even visceral dimension of linguistic relativism and poetic indeterminacy. Like many linguists, I was originally drawn to the field, in part, by the experience of hearing dialect differences and speaking different dialects (this mattering as much as languages). That a language is a different world is to a significant degree a matter of the nontranslatable music of language (as is dealt with explicitly in chapter 3 and in the purely linguistic concerns with dialect in chapter 4).

The fifth poem, "Kinship Alpha: Proto-Indo-European," brings together two ideas that are in many ways incompatible. The first is to compose a poem in the sounds, word patterns, and culture patterns associated with one particular modern Indo-European language, here American English. The second idea is to take as the content for such a poem the specific, anthropologically researched and established patterns, symbols, values—whatever—of a primitive, prehistoric, or otherwise exotic culture or subculture. The so-called Omaha kinship system of the Proto-Indo-Europeans and the idea of such a system are constructs or models of anthropologists and linguists. But they also correspond to a kind of kinship found in many parts of the world, as well as having intense analogues and resonances with our own experience of patrilineal kinship in many American families today. The integrity of such an inferred or reconstructed exotic universe in microcosm must be essentially maintained. Such a cultural poem is rare. It differs categorically from the sort of poem that is very common today where the exotica function as raw material for a poem that is primarily personal and, in its way, culture bound, since the internal relations between the symbols differ drastically from their internal relations within the exotic culture.

"Spinoza, I Love You" reflects my relation to the Jewish ritual and learning of my wife. Speaking more generally, sacred language and text, song and dance, genealogy, family and ethnic differences, history and cosmogony are melted into one experience that transcends the ritual source. At another level, the poem arises from the way the mind/body, reason/feeling, and other dichotomies were overridden by Spinoza.

The final poem, "The Master of Words," is a tribute to my father. Carl Friedrich, an anti-Nazi refugee and eventually a renowned political scientist, took great inspiration from American literature and the American political tradition; both excitements are reflected in his *The New Belief in the Common Man*. The excitements were saliently—at times I think primarily—linguistic/poetic. I remember, for example, how he savored Milton's "Thus spake the fiend / And of necessity, with tyrant's plea, / Excused his devilish deed." So impressed was I by these words that, aged fifteen, I carved them into the bark of a difficult-to-shinny poplar tree, forty feet above ground.

"The Master of Words" is meant to suggest my father's love struggle with language and limited but, within those limits, decisive mastery over many expressive, persuasive, and denotative resources of English. This struggle by an immigrant "Kraut Professor" in chauvinist New England grows into a metaphor for any poetic person and the wonders of his/her language. The poem suggests essential interdependencies between individual uniqueness, multilingualism, and cultural affiliation, and between linguistic-aesthetic integration and clinical aphasia, amnesia, and, ultimately, metaphysical chaos: when the poem was written, Alzheimer's disease was laying waste to Carl Friedrich (1900–1984).

I

Sketches for an Ode to
"The Yankee Clipper"

Joseph Paul DiMaggio
6′2″, 193 lbs., born in Martinez, CA

"They threw at his head a lot, especially when he first broke in."
"[Feller's curve] would come right at a right-handed hitter's head
then start to break and wind up at his knees for a strike.
Most of them moved away from it.

Not DiMaggio. He just stood there, watched it, and hit it hard."
"He could hit the ball and he wasn't afraid of the pitcher."
"He had this open stance . . . flat-footed . . . never waved the bat.
no stride into the ball; he would just hold back and crush it."
"He had this knack of hitting it the last split-second after it broke."

"When the chips were down and the big money was on the line."
"To hit in the clutch," with the doctor's bone spur:
"This guy did the operation. He did it all wrong.
He used a horrible incision and went into the heel the wrong way."
And DiMaggio was out until the crucial series against Boston . . .
                                        Single in the third.
Line drive homer in the seventh breaks up the game. The bench
    goes wild.
Single and second homer in the second game to win.
A homer in the third, and another out of the park.
"That had to be the greatest exhibition of pressure ball I ever saw."
And the streaks: 61 games with the Seals, and 56 with the Yankees
when every at bat after game 20 was "in the clutch"
and the country watched and read the front pages
until game 57 and Keltner's and Boudreau's saves.
DiMag: "Do you know if I got a hit I would have made ten
    thousand dollars?
The Heinz 57 people were following me."
"The greatest batting achievement of all," said Ted Williams.
"There isn't a record that will be harder to break than Joe's 56
    games."

Or the weird clutch—1942
ninth inning, two out, third strike, and the Yankees lose the World
    Series purse
but the catcher, Mickey Owen, misses the ball.
DiMag: "When order was restored it was my turn to bat.
    Casey was like a raging wild man.
    He poured over two strikes and I
    Singled off the next pitch."
"He was like that in the streak too . . .
a lot of those hits came the last time up . . .
I wish I had some records of the runs he drove in for us
in games after the seventh, eighth and ninth innings."

"He saw the faults the pitcher had and he would hit the ball."
"I asked and he said 'anticipation,' figuring the play before it
    happens."
"He had this marvelous sense of anticipation, he studied the game."
"Nobody ever studied the game more than Joe."
"He was a perfectionist."
"He was always trying to improve himself."
"The best thing DiMaggio had was his head."
"He never forgot anything." "Joe never made a mental mistake."
"Caught once in over a thousand miles on the base paths."
"In all the years I knew him he was never thrown out stretching."
"The finest fielding outfielder in the toughest center field."
"No one who ever saw DiMaggio glide back for a fly ball . . .
nobody in baseball could come in on a line drive like Joe."
"He loved to play shallow . . . best throwing arm in baseball."
"The most skillful of all players in their opening years."
"It's the way he played, the style, the dedication."
"He was just a complete ballplayer." "He was by himself."
Voted "the greatest living player" in 1966
"I guess he never had any weakness."
"A ballplayer's ballplayer. He could throw on a dime."
"The most graceful player of all time." The Yankee Clipper.

"The thing about DiMaggio is he always gave a thousand percent
    every game."
"I was cocky, confident . . . but I kept it inside myself, inside
    the shell."
"Joe is probably the most self-effacing guy I have ever met."
"A very lonely man at times." "An introvert in those days."
    "Tense."
Thirty half-cups of coffee a day, one or two packs of Camels.
"He never seemed to be able to let loose and just enjoy himself."
"Joe wasn't a guy you could kid around with in the training room."
"I don't know if anybody really knows Joe DiMaggio."
"He had a toughness and a coldness with strangers, sort of guards
    himself
but all that seems to break down with the kids. They adore him."
DiMag: "There might be a kid in the stands, or five or ten
who had never seen me play or would never see me play again.
I burned in the belly to be the best there was for them
to leave them with a good memory of me."

"[When he came up to bat] guys would yell, 'Dago, Wop, Guinea,'
Joe never moved."
"His parents only spoke Italian
and that had something to do with his shyness."
"His parents were very strict, especially with money."
"His parents were hermits, you never knew what went on inside
     that house"
with the five DiMaggio brothers, four to be pros, three in the
     majors.
"He used his first World Series money to buy his mother a new
     home."
"He was always inviting you to these Italian restaurants."
" 'When you eat with the Dago, the Dago pays,' he'd say, and pick
     up the tab"
for brothers, team-mates, best friends:
Gomez, Lazzeri, Boraschino, Martin, Lombardi, and Solotaire.
"Joe Solotaire would constantly provide him with beautiful
     showgirls to date."
"The last American knight," with his Dago honor, and fear of
     shame.

Joe DiMaggio never wanted to look ridiculous," to be "the hero in a
     farce."
"DiMaggio would never do anything that would embarrass anybody
     else."
"The perfect gentleman." "He wouldn't do anything cheap."
"I can describe him with one word: class."
"Few people knew what a team man he was."
"If you embarrass him he'll cut you off dead
but if he's a friend he is a very loyal guy."

"When she had that crackup, she turned to him."
"He was a tough cookie and she could depend on him."
Later: "He wanted her buried with dignity." "A sense of purity."

2

I thought I saw some Eskimos—

fishing in Chicago
down from the Playboy Tower by the chess pavillion:

a high cheek-boned woman, and a small boy with a carton
squealing and hopping around in the icy waves
while his father whirled and cast a barbed trident
far, far out, then hauled it in again.

They hadn't caught a fish
and I'm not sure they were planning for a catch
by coming down to join with the spring waters—
any more than they hankered to peer at their own features
in the choppy wavelets.

Nor was it trout and rock bass
they'd mainly look for in a still pool, but sharp laughter
and the sounds of Eskimo (or was it Japanese?)
to match whatever lies beneath the mirror surfaces.

3

I wanted to pass through the drift prairies
after the blue-flowered flax and bronzed wheat
had died away and yielded their cracked stems
to the whiteness of North Dakota—not
empty, not a void land staring up
like the unclosed eyes of a pioneer
slain by the Sioux, spread-eagled, alone—
but prairie peopled by sagebrush and grass
that the morning sun's rays make crystaline
and each tumbleweed dancing downward
becomes a still gesture of the possible.
This sagebrush, unique as I,
or you, will not melt like the memory
of some echo, the last nerve in a brain.
It will stay like that Sioux with a scarred nose

they wouldn't let get on. "You been drinkin'."
He stood flapping his tattered black coat
outside the Paragon Terminal Cafe
outside Dickinson, North Dakota.

4

Where does it end, where does it begin?
With Artemis, the twitter of siskins?
Or St. Chrysostom's hymn to the Virgin
during Easter when the choir's colors
pour down to echo on the Russian icons?
Or the warbling of my baby daughter
month after month—toward language?
Or with Taráscan mothers' lullabies
and how they might spin into a poem?
Or Sappho's songs to her one little girl,
her vowels weaving within Mandelstam
with Russian song, the whispering of countesses,
the tender *zh*'s, the feminine-rounded *o*'s?
. . . I want the tune of all languages,
the four tones in a classic T'ang stanza,
the nine tones in a fisherman's conversation,
the music of all language filtering in
to a world listener.

5

Kinship Alpha:
Proto-Indo-European

*pətēr   father, father, father
           horn-hard-handed
           household-holder
           giver of daughters
           tamer of horses
           warrior
           elder in my town and clan

māter   mother, mother, mother
a womb for our clan
not wife till you bore
me or my brother
mistress to my sisters, and to nieces by my father's brothers
mistress to their washing, winnowing, winter's weaving
working windrows through summers and the anguish of harvest

sūnūs   son, little son, son
seed of our clan, of semen sprung
sapling of ash, ash-spear holder
young steer now, then sun-steer strong
horse-stealer. Stole your bride!
riding hard, lashing hard
laid her down in our home

dhugətēr   daughter, daughter, born to be lost
calyx of matrix, mother-nurtured
laughing with sisters by lightest
dawn, with the girls of our clan.
Heifer!
You danced, ran
raked, laundered, milked, gleaned—till your wedding

bhrātēr   brothers, brothers, brothers
and you, sons of my father's brothers—all my brothers
blood avengers, you men and age-mates in my patri-clan
youngest brother: heir to our hearth
protect its sparks and embers
elder brother: teacher in work and war
right hand to our father: leader

swesōr   sister of the rising moon
womb of our own, then gone too soon
woman we give for the wife I get
with exchanges in cows for our unknown brides
blood and trust for lust and bondage
leave our home, lose our name
labor in exile, spare us shame

*g*ʷ*enā*
cattle-priced companion, wife
cowed witch of love
veiled you came
to serve and be tamed
bear and suckle my sons
in my space
my hearth and house

snusos
woman of my son, son's woman
kinswoman by wedding with a youth of my blood
two families' sinew, and tendon of two clans
but unclean, alien
blood, you
serve and tempt me, mushroom-picker!
how you balance your water jug!

gemətēr
groom of my sister or a daughter
wooer and buyer, gift-giver, or taker
took her, or raped her, doomed her
before our messengers went with requests
before the wedding that binds us now
to a foreign home and a foreign town
blood wedding? all weddings are

awos: mother's brother or mother's father
father and giver of my mother, or
her brother, avenger of her honor, my favoring "male mother"
you older men of her patri-clan
I stand here, your nephew, *nepos*, son of your sister/daughter
give me presents
foster and raise me during summer visits

6

Spinoza, I Love You

It is this delicacy in ritual I can hardly stand,
Each syllable balanced by poets in the desert,
The dignity of each letter stalking down to us
To form these simple songs of praise to the One,
To Life, to the World around us tnat we know—
Where every morsel means like the songs we sing,
Where parsley in salt water is the tears of sadness,
Horseradish is bitterness, apples are bricks of toil,
Unleavened bread and a shank of lamb are liberation
We consume together in our holy family.
                                        Candlelight.
And now the fine contralto of her voice raises
Our five-year-old in lavender up, out of her chair
To dance and swing and pump her wild little arms,
Pulsing like kibutzniks or bedouins under god's sky—
On our linoleum as I join her and we partners circle
The floor faster and faster within the archaic words
That are within us now as they spoke to our forebears.
Genealogies rise up in Silesia and Lithuania and Alsacia.
Even my Sephardic Jewish, bankrupt mother's father's father
Lives with us on this Passover Seder in a family kitchen.

7

The Master of Words

My old father has a German accent, OK
but he was a master of our English words
that he hunted out like a prospector
to prize, holding them up on our long strolls—
"Look! a golden scarab from Egypt, a crown jewel!"—
and gave to us at the family supper table
until my Yankee mother exclaimed, "Achim, please!
You've been saying 'wizened' and 'minatory' for weeks!"

Germany was his mother, but America his wife.
He collected words for her diadem
from Thoreau, Jefferson, Tom Paine,
from "his" farmers in Vermont—"The Common Man,"
and polished and tested out each cutting gem
that despite, and because of, his tainted accent
created conviction in the blasé Harvard sophisticates
who surged up—every year—after his last class
to clap and render standing praise
while he shuffled together his notes and smiled,
then hurried to the exit with an Old World handwave. . . .

Today he sits, trapped in an old people's home:
TV's, walls, speechless oldies, nurses,
his phrases piecemeal, strained out in slow motion
like his trembly hands barely spooning up his yogurt:
"I failed . . . never wrote a great book . . .
what I recall about Paul . . . he was small . . .
heard a stanza once . . . could give it all back . . .
you get lonely here . . .
winter here will be cold and wintry . . .
I worry about the children and Mumsey . . .
it's no use, but I do . . ."

like smoke seeking the suck of wind outside the portal
or sinking lower and rising toward the margins,
or like a dying bear, cold gnawing his fat
he sits, head crooked to one side
strapped in his wheelchair
the master of words

8

Linguistic Relativity and
the Order-to-Chaos Continuum

> Rationalists, wearing square hats,
> Think, in square rooms
> Looking at the floor,
> Looking at the ceiling.
> They confine themselves
> To right-angled triangles.
> If they tried rhomboids,
> Cones, waving lines, ellipses—
> As for example, the ellipse of the half moon—
> Rationalists would wear sombreros.
>
> **WALLACE STEVENS,** *"Six Significant Landscapes"*

This chapter is my second extended argument in favor of a hypothesis of linguistic relativity, to wit: that any natural language such as English massively shapes, channels, filters, and otherwise determines the individual imagination. The first argument, in chapter 3, shows how analogical, associative, and connotative patterns—particularly in poetry and "poetic language"—are the locus of differences between languages and hence the focus of linguistic relativity. Like the previous chapter this one is critical of extreme versions of the "cognitive-referential" position and contends that poetic and associative meanings are more comprehensive than that position acknowledges.

The present chapter is, then, continuous with the third. It is also discontinuous in that it approaches linguistic relativity at a more philosophical level, through consideration of yet other abstract and often paradoxical dimensions such as linearity and instantaneity. It deals with cumulative complexity and tries to show how this complexity makes any one language unique and poorly transformable into another. Particular attention is given to a dimension that has been widely ignored until very recently, namely, degrees of order and lack of order—including chaos—in language.

GENERAL THEORY

> This division of territory between science and philosophy was
> not a simple business. . . .
>
> A. N. WHITEHEAD, *Science and the Modern World*

General theory constitutes an integration of ideas about some body
of knowledge, both established knowledge and recent, problematical
experiments and discoveries—for instance, that color terms are controlled by a specific part of the brain, as Geschwind and Fusillo have
argued. General theory is especially sensitive to ideas that don't fit
current doctrines and to what Whitehead called "hard, stubborn
facts" (such as the outer limits on memory). It is also sensitive to
knowledge and insights from personal experience, deductive reasoning, and aesthetic apprehension. General theory differs from theory
that is almost exclusively centered on specific hypotheses, methods,
and patterns of heuristic simplification—as illustrated by the intense
clusterings of scientists around often minute empirical problem
areas (such as cross-cousin marriage or "the laryngeal hypothesis").
   General theory is relatively free to associate and speculate. Nor
is it bound by the immediate operationalism of the "let me go home
right away and try it on my data" variety. General theory veers freely
into what used to be called the metaphysical—which I prefer to call
the metaphenomenal (to avoid the issue of the physical versus the
nonphysical). General theory overlaps with "interpretation" in colloquial usage and in philosophy, but too imperfectly for these to
serve as alternate terms. General theory connects freely with the generic ethical, political, aesthetic, and mythic-religious ideas of its
time, partly because "objective" and "impersonal" positions always
turn out, anyway, to reflect and be influenced by larger intellectual
climates and contexts, and vice versa.

DISCRETENESS/CONTINUITY

here begin a series of contrasts

> You're searching, Joe,
> For things that don't exist; I mean beginnings.
> Ends and beginnings—there are no such things.
> There are only middles.
>
> ROBERT FROST, *"In the Home Stretch"*

> a theory of discontinuous existence is required . . .
>
> A. N. WHITEHEAD, *Science and the Modern World*

One of our primary intuitions of language and all other experience is of an essential continuity. The theoretical *assumption* of overall continuousness is suggested, in particular, by the experience of language use in context, by the way language is learned and forgotten, by the clines and series in dialect studies, and by many of the facts about languages in contact. The continuousness of language variables is also central to many linguistic models, in phonetics, and in syntax. In the latter subfield, for example, the most fruitful and realistic view of the ordering of the verb and other meaningful elements is often by frequencies, or "percent rules," no matter how detailed and precise we get in establishing syntactic structures. Even in the entrenched heartland of categorical "either/or" grammar, namely Sanskrit grammar, we find that Vedic Sanskrit syntax is ordered in the main by percent rules and actually has few strictly obligatory ones; Classical Sanskrit prose, although more regular, is also marked by many statistical rules of all kinds at all levels. Linguistic units, even the terms for colors and kinsmen, are fuzzy at the edges.

Our primary experience and the theoretical assumption of continuity are rivaled or exceeded by that of the separability of units and levels from each other. Awareness of the separateness of sounds, words, phrases, songs, dialects, and other language units must date back to the Upper Paleolithic and certainly arises in children before the ability to speak. Opposition and the invariance of such oppositional relations are probably felt by all speakers of a language as a major dimension of their experience.

We can "handle" the realia of discreteness with *analytical* invariants such as the distinctive feature in phonology or in the anthropology of categories; for example, the sacred versus the profane, right versus left, and the like. We have fascinating and probative experiments on binary structure combined with continuity in the

are these comparable?

meaning of adjectives—meanings that correspond to such idiomatic oppositions as those between "yellow belly" and "the red badge of courage." A combination of considerations, then, appears to justify our assuming a considerable degree of discreteness.

The roles of discreteness and continuity have been distorted in various ways. One is to relegate continuity and quantifiable phenomena generally to behavior or history, despite the fact that a set of continuous variables can hold in a steady state over long periods. For example, immigration quotas or a complex of rules for intermarriage between ethnic groups may include some frequencies, not only in the theory of the sociologist, but also in the natives' perception of the matter ("we marry/get wives from *them* every few years just to keep up the connection"). On the other hand, a qualitative, either/or rule of marriage (or of pronunciation) can shift by a leap that resembles the sudden and instantaneous catalysis in chemistry, that is, without a quantitative, statistically definable process. Or a gradual, quantitative change may suddenly shift to a qualitative one.

Nor is it tenable to say that continuous variables are more concrete or (which amounts to the same thing) that they are the tokens of some more abstract, symbolic, or otherwise superior level. In fact, contrary to most abstract linguistics and symbolic anthropology, it is often continuous, quantifiable variables involving small differences of measurement that are superordinate. For example, the frequency rule for marriage suggested above usually entails or subcategorizes actors who are themselves categorized in either/or terms. In the same way, a continuous or scalar phonological rule may subcategorize an either/or phonetic one.

The way discreteness and continuity are combined can be illustrated by almost any syntactic or semantic field: for example, in English, terms for colors or for basic emotions. The chromatic meaning of any color term, such as "green," or of any term for an emotion, such as "jealousy," is continuous in that the boundaries of their meanings are fuzzy and shade off into other areas. Where does green shade into blue, where does jealousy shade into envy? Yet, as Berlin and Kay have shown, for any speaker (or culture) there is a central core or focus such that any instance of the focus will be classed with the term, and the term can always be applied to a certain restricted, unambiguous area "well within the fuzz." Between these focal or unambiguous areas there are definite relations, and the total set of such relations between relations constitutes a structure—open-ended, imperfect, but still a structure. This simple lexical example could be supplemented by much more complex ones from language and culture.

The continuousness and discontinuousness of language at all levels and at all times resemble the imagination itself, which in one of its distillate forms—the dream—includes images as fixed and discrete as letters of the alphabet and others as continuous as flight. In this duality language also resembles the biological world, whose Mendelian laws are combined with the continuous drift of mutation and genetic decay. It also resembles the physical world, with its continuous fields of energy and electricity, coexisting with the discrete structure of quarks and of the Pythagorean Theorem in its modern applications (i.e., as generalized and used by Einstein in his formula for four-dimensional space).

But the paradox of continuity and discontinuity is peculiarly basic to language, and it is the governing formal principle for all of language's other dimensions as these intersect with each other. The interworkings of continuity and discontinuity increase the complexity and therefore the uniqueness and nontranslatability of any one language (and of other cultural codes and communicational processes). They also decrease the theoretical value of any formal determinism, or of the sort of general linguistic relativism which argues that languages are largely intelligible and translatable in terms of a "universal calculus."

BEHAVIOR/"UNDERLYING" MEANING

> Strange and hard that paradox true I give
> Objects gross and the unseen soul are one.
> **WALT WHITMAN**, *Leaves of Grass*

> The surface is not clear—nor the depths obscure.
> *Tao Te Ching*

A second primary dimension of our experience of language is one that ranges between, for example, the superficial behavior of naming a yellow primrose yellow, and, on the other hand, imaging the rose at the end of Dante's *Paradise* XXX.124–126: "Into the yellow of the sempiternal rose/Which dilates, rises rank on rank, breathes forth/In incenses of praise to the forever vernal sun." An awareness of the differences between superficial labeling and deeper meaning is essential when one is inferring a delicate structure in either area.

The opposition between behavior and deeper meaning is signaled in scholarly fields by such dyads of terms—some of them red herrings—as "evaluation by a participant" versus "observed behavior," society (societal behavior) versus culture (cultural structure), social process versus cultural system, or *la parole* versus *la langue* or "performance" versus "competence." Note the tendency for persons mainly interested in the deeper meanings in language and culture to associate these meanings with "structure" or order rather than with lack of order or anything chaotic; for them, meaning seems equal, or at least quintessential, to order—and vice versa.

The above couplets of technical terms, together with their relations to behavioral regularity and to deeper structures, have been beclouded by reification, that is, the attribution of a more concrete meaning to a set of terms than they in fact have; reification is in some ways the opposite of reduction. Because of this reification, many students of language and culture come to assume that some sort of clean and straight line can be drawn between a dirty zone of observable, statistical, audible, behavioral reality and a dialectically opposed realm of clean-cut, inferred, mental, deeper or higher, structured reality. In fact, no such line or chasm exists. Speech and so-called social processes are always significantly categorical, while no matter how deep we go, cultural and linguistic structures are always significantly continuous—they have to be because they are constantly in flux, changing. Thus, what may exist as a superficial and observable set of options for one person may constitute a presupposed, densely fixed gridiron of rules for another. One person's competence (deep system) may be closely analogous to another's behavior, and this potential commutation holds both for two grammarians and for two ordinary participants in a single culture. Comparatively speaking, what is rigidly categorical in one language and culture may be relatively loose, superficial, and random in another: compare the patterns of pronominal usage in nineteenth-century Germany and seventeenth-century France (as reflected in Molière).

The greater proportion, if not all, of language and culture is played out in middle zones that simultaneously comprise large measures of behavior and of deeper levels of structured meaning. It is more difficult to transform between two such complexly mixed systems than between *either* two descriptions of behavior or two simple algorithms (which latter could conceivably be treated as literal functions of each other). Thus the paradox of structure and behavior bears on the issue of complexity and hence of relativity. The paradox has been compounded by intersecting it with the following dimension.

COMMUNAL/GENERIC INDIVIDUAL/UNIQUE INDIVIDUAL
3 - way

> Instead, therefore, of arguing from a supposed objectivity of
> culture to the problem of individual variation, we shall, for
> certain kinds of analysis, have to proceed in the opposite
> direction.
>
> EDWARD SAPIR, *"Why Cultural Anthropology Needs the Psychiatrist"*

Our third dimension at one of its poles, that of the unique individual, corresponds to such universal experiences as learning to speak a language in childhood or harboring thoughts to oneself. It can be productive by itself when, for example, one is studying the role of language in symbolizing the personality of the unique individual. It is illustrated by the way the resources of the Tarascan language are synthesized in the intonations of one potter, Emilio Alejos, or by the denial by someone of what all the other natives report, leading, invaluably, to our understanding of a tabooed zone of discourse. Finally, it is illustrated by the role of the linguist's personal experience in constructing a general theory.

The pole of the unique individual contrasts with the generic individual, the "ideal speaker-hearer" whose system is typically inferred by means of introspection and forms produced by the linguist. Both the unique and the generic individual contrast with language at the communal or cultural level: for example, with "the system" of Mexican-American English in Los Angeles, or "the system" of Proto-Indo-European as reconstructed by the comparativist. The various contrasts between these aspects of language are suggested by a great number of opposed technical terms, such as idiolect versus dialect, ideal speaker-hearer versus *la langue*, and egocentric versus sociocentric. None of these dyads of terms means quite the same thing, of course, since each has emerged from distinct contexts. Further, the terms or dyads are combined in various ways: the term of community plus that of structure, for example, yields *la langue* to the linguist and one concept of "culture" to the anthropologist. The overwhelming majority of language research, incidentally, is in terms of the generic individual (e.g., transformational-generative linguistics) or of the social-communal (sociolinguistics).

The major reality, of course, is the continuous one between (and out beyond) the polar extremes of the unique individual and the communal-cultural. These realities, both of which are mental or psychological, contextualize each other to a significant degree. In other words, an abstract community or an ideal speaker-hearer is not to be separated theoretically from the unique individuals who learn and use and create language in specific and generic contexts. The point of view that focuses exclusively on the communal or on the generic individual—the one that typifies most current research—may be a useful heuristic but should not be taken at the cost of a reified distortion. A stronger position would include the generic and communal-cultural process and emphasize its interaction with process in unique persons.

SUBJECTIVE/OBJECTIVE

> We are finally led to believe that laws of nature we formulate mathematically in quantum theory deal no longer with the particles themselves but with our knowledge of the elementary particles.
>
> WERNER HEISENBERG, *Physics and Philosophy*

The dimension of the individual and communal overlaps with the basic continuity between the subjective and the objective. Disregard of this continuity has contributed, for example, to the subjectivism in abstract linguistics and in some symbolic anthropology. Subjectivism, when dogmatic, is as fallacious as the earlier positivism, which located reality in an external world. Reality includes both the unique "I" and the external world of culture, organic life and the physical universe, both the partly ordering imagination and the partly ordered world around us.

The position that bridges subjective and objective is analogous to the view of most contemporary physicists, who concur that the observer is also always a participant; there is no universe without its observer nor any observer who is not part of the universe of description. The main qualification to the analogy is that our problem as students of language is more complex in the sense that, even when introspecting, we have to consider not one but two observer-participants: the linguist-analyst and the native speaker-hearer.

More illuminating than the analogy with physics is one with a poem that can be read at once objectively, as a description of something "external," and as a highly personal, intimate, and even erotic projection of the poet's person. The subjectivity of such poetry can even include two or more subjective points of view—as in the ambiguity between the first, second, and third persons in many Early

Tamil, T'ang Chinese, or Japanese haiku poems. When we translate such poetry our equation must include not only the source and target languages, the respective poetic languages, and the two poems, but four participant-observers—and, indeed, a half dozen or more other major variables.

LOGICO-REFERENTIAL AND ASSOCIATIVE MEANING

Ripeness is all.
WILLIAM SHAKESPEARE, *King Lear* 5.2

denote / connote

Literal meanings are packaged commodities for passive consumers.
NORMAN O. BROWN, *Love's Body*

We can say that language has functions without committing ourselves disastrously to some narrow and exclusive functionalism. In this sense, part of the work of language is to help us cope with the material and natural worlds, with social and psychological problems. Here, language symbolizes propositions and ideas in various practical, minimal, or at least highly economical ways: we need to talk about prejudice and carburetors, sodium chloride and red. These practical meanings are of primary concern to most people in most cultures some or most of the time.

The practical workings of language also require such minimal grammatical meanings as the past tense. And they require a minimal logical symbolism that has to include, for instance, negation, class inclusion, conjunction, and various kinds of levels of noncontradiction within discourse. The logical and syntactic operations that I have in mind differ greatly from one language to the next in their status and frequency. For example, Homeric Greek has more overt logical operators and they are more frequent than is the case in Classical Hebrew. Similarly, we find enormous differences between speakers of the same language when it comes to the frequency and status of minimal grammatical and logical meanings.

The overall aspect of language that I have in mind is labelled referential, denotative, logico-referential, or referential-semantic. This logical and referential universe often is equated with the context-free, but it doesn't have to be. Logico-referential sets can be strictly associated with different contexts.

Despite the practical importance of logical and referential lan-

guage, language is *never* exclusively or even in large part a strictly logical code of univocal signs. (By "univocal" is meant the unreal world where one form has one and only one meaning, and vice versa. It is "unreal" because it does not obtain even in the natural sciences, where the logical positivists got it.)

Language in all of its symbolizations and networks always suggests and connotes meanings that may be fundamental without being either particularly logical or particularly practical. Its symbols, from the specific sound to the syntactic formula, always have multiple values that are to some degree integrated and synthesized into a multidimensional whole. We will never really understand the motivation for all this complexity, much of it playful or redundant, but it surely bespeaks deep needs of the imagination, particularly aesthetic ones, and just as basic needs for ambiguity, redundancy, and simple repetition in communications.

The sort of language in question is called connotative, poetic, associational, and secondary—which is misleading. There is nothing secondary about such language. On the contrary, its associative network includes logico-referential meanings. For example, the meaning of "shoe" as a type of protective covering for the foot is part of a larger meaning that includes horseshoes, the shoes of a wheel casing, and so forth—and this by only one particular type of metaphor. If the processes of the imagination are taken to include the twenty volumes that psychologists agree we dream every night, and the impractical thoughts, daydreams, and conversations of the day, then the associative universe would surely be more comprehensive than the logico-referential one. On the other hand, the algorithm for logico-referential meaning is not a subsystem of the analogical system; it is necessary to differentiate between language and the analyst's language.

We never find pure reference, even in artificial metalanguages, symbolic logic, or mathematics, because even these fields have a poetic aureola that may be decisive in theory formation: "French mathematics," for example, entails certain aesthetic connotations and standards of elegance in proof. Even grossly referential or assiduously scientific language has a poetic aspect.

Just as pure reference is a figment of the imagination, so there is no such thing as purely poetic or suggestive language; poetry also refers. Coleridge, intensely poetic as he was, aloof from the practical, also always refers: *Kubla Khan* refers to an imaginable world of images. By the same token the near-nonsense of other poetry—for example, "Jabberwocky"—evokes images that are typical and primary for most readers; indeed, some of the fun and beauty of this masterpiece derives from the way it refers while pretending not to. We must recall, in this connection, that meaning in poetry as in the rest of language is partly probabilistic, and that definiteness and precision in language are always matters of degree. Even suggestiveness in poetry can be intensified until it approximates reference; a good example would be Shakespeare's "Ripeness is all." Here, poetry equates with music, and music, as Langer says, is a "morphology of feeling," that is, a structured process of musical forms that corresponds to a structured process of psychological ones. These musical and poetic forms are not illogical; they are logical and alogical.

That language both refers and suggests has been obscured by the academic polarization between the two functions. Logicians, syntacticians, and many symbolic ethnoscientists come down hard on the side of simple referential schemes, while poeticians, Prague Schoolers, and most symbolic anthropologists pay rather more attention to the poetic side of things. This academic polarization has obscured the degree to which language is *both* referential and poetic and how the overwhelming mass of language use has both obvious referential and poetic aspects most of the time. To stay with familiar examples, both Whorf's "gorgeous, rapture, soul, and star dust" and Carroll's "Twas brillig and the slithy toves" could not be translated/transformed into another language without great loss of information and cognitive as well as emotional meanings. In sum, there is a pervasive continuousness between poetry and reference in language, and this is another source for the uniqueness of languages and the relative untranslatability between them.

The simultaneous double function of both referring and suggesting is perhaps the most important of the many functions that constitute the multifunctional nature of language and communication summarized. These functions include that of referring back to the codes of the language being used, the so-called metalinguistic function—as is illustrated by this sentence (about functions in language) that is just ending. They also include the poetic function in the narrow sense of referring back upon or "highlighting" or "foregrounding" the message itself; that is, the form of the message. This structuralist meaning of "poetic" differs, of course, from the more comprehensive and colloquial one that I have been following, where "poetic" or "associative" contrasts with but, at another level, *includes* reference and similar basic meaning.

A particularly basic function is the emotive or expressive one that involves the attitudes, feelings, and other subjective states of the speaker *and* of the hearer *and* of other parties to the speech event. (In other words, the emotive function should not be limited to the speaker.) The emotive or expressive function has a strong connection with the poetic one, with which it should not be confused or identified. The main content of this relation is that the emotions are the *main* source or driving force for the poetic (in either of the senses used above) and hence are more powerful, or "deeper." "Main" because there are other driving forces, and the poetic function can be largely independent of the emotive one—as when motivated by the code ("metrical consideratons") or by context (that dictates a formulaic expression) and so forth.

LINEARITY/INSTANTANEITY

> Then felt I like some watcher of the skies
> When a new planet swims into his ken
> Or like stout Cortez when with eagle eyes
> He stared at the Pacific. . . .
> JOHN KEATS, *"On First Reading Chapman's Homer"*

Another dimension arises from the way we speak through time, from the fact that sound segments, in the now classic cliché, are like beads on a string or a chain. Moreover, not only histories and recipes but also myths and other less obvious kinds of discourse are acted out along some narrative line; language is linear. This has been a cornerstone of diverse linguistic positions ever since Saussure adequately weighed and also somewhat exaggerated its significance. "Somewhat exaggerated" because in many ways there is no underlying linearity: is the underlying predicator initial or final? Often there is no clear motivation for linearity except a surface rule. The imagination itself is nonlinear to a large extent, as the workings of analogy suggest and as is congruous with the neurological evidence on the workings of the right hemisphere in particular. Time-consciousness itself is largely nonlinear. Language is nonlinear in part.

Specific kinds of language, such as short lyric, are notably nonlinear in part; their symbols, although pronounced serially, are held in the imagination as a totality. When the symbols are deployed spatially on a page they appear more or less simultaneously, and the memory of them endures in a tangible, nonlinear form. Similarly, a word, a line, even a stanza in Chinese characters can, as a whole, leap into the eye all at once—shortcutting most of the linear aspects of its organization.

The relation of linear to nonlinear is thus quite complicated and paradoxical. In the audible chain of conversation, for example, some sounds will be imagined before others are being articulated, and this anticipatory imagining will affect what is being said. In the same way, the short-term memory of what has just been articulated will affect the present act. This high-speed cybernetic scanning up ahead and backwards along the imagined sound stream presupposes both the (linear) stream and also an essentially nonlinear or alinear monitoring and synthesis of that stream as a field or simultaneously apprehended structure.

Linearity has to be qualified yet further. I am thinking of what I call multiple tracking in language use, the more or less simultaneous imagining (e.g., encoding and decoding) of two or more strings of messages, whether this involves two or more languages or two or more trains of thought. One of my best Tarascan Indian assistants, while answering my questions about the dictionary, would typically follow in his mind the lyrics to the Mexican song that was being broadcast loudly over the village loudspeaker *and*, intermittently, diverse strands of thought about the daily cycle that he had been persuaded to neglect for the sake of a linguistic interview *and*, intermittently, diverse strains of memory that were triggered by the words in my dictionary. Obviously my faithful Indian was not actively pursuing all of these all the time—that would be not only improbable but impossible—but he was following two or even more a lot of the time, according to both his own intuition and my judgment of his awareness of the tracks in question. This man was illiterate. He was brainy but I don't think he was a genius, nor would I call him insane.

Many individuals are extraordinarily action-oriented or "nonverbal," or they live in a world that is so immediate in its practical demands that daydreaming and multiple tracking are drastically limited. But the basic experience of multiple coding and imagining remains normal to some extent for most speakers and dominant in the language of some; it also typifies many conversations as well as states of confusion and "not meaning what one said." The more language tracks being followed, the less likely that any one of them is linear—simply because they connect up with each other and loop together and back and forth at various points. The more tracks, the more alinear monitoring is in play. Multiple tracking is part of the generic human process of simultaneously handling several levels of information while focusing on only one or two at a time (the focus may shift frequently). Multiple tracking, then, which is ignored by linguistics, illustrates how general theory should take account of ordinary experience as well as the established knowledge of science.

Nonlinearity is well illustrated by other examples from verbal art, notably in oral traditions, but also wherever composition or performance is oral. To begin with a minuscule example: someone who has memorized a nursery rhyme or a TV commercial knows it as a point or a uniform field, not as linked fragments. More compelling is the genesis of a poem, of *Kubla Khan* in the imagination of Coleridge or of the *Sonnets to Orpheus* in that of Rilke. We have impeccable documentation of the birth of theories and of monumental compositions in science and art—one ought to mention Handel's *Messiah*—which came as explosions or instantaneous illuminations that were then unpackaged along various dimensions of which the linear is but one, and before which the empirical fact of linearity pales in significance. In these cases the great complexities of a poem or of a piece of music were somehow telescoped and concentrated on one psychological point. Of course, the intention or goal of linearity must not be confused with the performance or existence of linearity.

To those who protest against generalizing from creations of genius in our own tradition, with possible overtones of Romanticism, one might point to monumental and instantaneous creation of sections of his great vision by Chief Black Elk of the Oglala Sioux tribe and the many other well-established cases of instantaneous realization/creation by other shaman-poets among the American Indians. To those who then protest that one shouldn't generalize from poets or shamans, one could answer that these vast, personally original structures are no more complex than the unique, individually built command that fluent speakers always have of the genius of their mother tongue. This incomprehensibly complex mother tongue is known more or less "all at once" and any part can be brought into play more or less simultaneously. In other words, and this is un-Romantic, genius is a matter of degree.

ORIENTATION (MORE OR LESS)

> Humming birds and humming moths are so remarkably alike
> in habits and functional operation that they are often mistaken
> for each other if seen only from a distance. . . . The rule that
> all of life's opportunities tend to be followed has exceptions.
>
> GEORGE GAYLORD SIMPSON, *The Meaning of Evolution*

The paradox that language is simultaneously both linear and punctual (or fieldlike) is interconnected with paradoxical dimensions of language evolution, with change over long time spans. Much of this change is by structured shifts or a statistically ordered drift in a certain direction; for example, the unfolding of a phonology as it is described in many historical phonologies, or the pervasive restructuring of the semantics of a political rhetoric. Systems demonstrably tend.

An argument for goal-orientedness and drift in language or culture is always necessarily circular in part, since one is in the position of describing what happened and then asserting that it had to happen that way. But the circularity is only partial, because it is just as obvious that, in cases of change, there are significant differences in the degree of motivation, localization, and regularity or orderliness; some cases of change and some types of process are probably more ordered than others, more goal-directed. That is one reason why, in linguistics as in biology, we are persuaded to the assumption of teleonomy. Far from randomness vitiating teleonomy, it is differential randomness that provides evidence for it.

Such differential teleonomy must be distinguished from the extreme teleology of many linguists and anthropologists, which saddles us with false assumptions. On the one hand, we are told that "language is a system in which everything holds together," that is, that there is a totalistic, synchronic teleology. This persists in the currently fashionable doctrine of "totally rule-governed behavior" in synchronic studies. On the other hand, we are told that a subsystem in language tends in some particular direction that, implicitly, is necessary or preordained. Syntactic structures, for example, are said to tend toward certain ideal types such as Subject-Verb-Object (SVO). Teleology also has been proclaimed, if often unintentionally, by the many sociolinguists who focus on a few relatively discernible cases— which may border on being serendipities—of language change that is motivated by correlations with social variables. Yet more extremely teleological is the generativists' claim that the logical order of rules at one time will recapitulate the temporal order of changes up to that time. Such widespread teleology in linguistics resembles the notions of unilinear evolution in biology, from which some of it draws some of its inspiration. It is likewise rooted, as will be discussed below, in assumptions that are atavistically theological—which is one reason I have been using the older and more pejorative term "teleology" rather than "teleonomy."

Contrary to strictly ordered teleology, we may assume that process in language is variously (and paradoxically) ordered, and unordered. The lack of order may involve the unpredictability of the shape of a river boundary, or some other external fact such as contact with a particular foreign language in the aftermath of war; an influx of words with a feature such as glottalization may cause that feature to acquire phonemic status for all words in the receiving language. Or consider the vicissitudes of Russian kinship terminology and values between the Tsarist and Soviet periods, a time span that witnessed, successively, the emancipation of the serfs, cataclysmic land reform, uniquely rapid industrialization, war, revolution, and sovietization, with consequently high levels of free variation and confusion in kinship and other semantic fields (that has since sorted itself out and settled down again).

In other cases some of the movement of language resembles neither the ebb and flow of the tides nor an underlying, consistent current (Sapir's drift), but rather the aimless slopping back and forth and up and down of any large body of water, the rattling of dozens of stones in a box, or Brownian (random) motion in physics. I see no reason why language should differ from the rest of the world in not being in part significantly unordered and nonteleonomic.

In light of the above we are led to a position close to the current one of biological evolutionists. More biologists are keenly aware of the falsity of the ad hoc reasoning that supports unilinear evolution or otherwise totally necessitated evolution. My favorite example here is the saber-toothed tiger and the Irish elk, and the contention, now debunked, that they perished because of the specific fact that their teeth and antlers, respectively, got too big and cumbersome. Biological theorists such as Simpson recognize that evolution is far from predictable or explicable as the measured and geometrical unfolding of some rational plan, or in terms of mechanisms such as adaptation—to say nothing of the survival of the fittest. On the contrary, they emphasize the degree of unpredictability and the role of random drift, particularly in small populations, and of traits that are adaptively neutral—as practically all specific linguistic traits are, when taken in isolation, granting the obvious sociolinguistic exceptions. Biological evolution by random walk is an important, possibly dominant, mode of evolution; the probabilities in a random walk can of course be predicted—but with considerable variations in accuracy.

There is, on the other hand, overwhelming evidence for the more or less systematic unfolding of the formal potentials of a language. The unfolding within any one subsystem interacts with unfoldings in some of the others, and all of these internally motivated unfoldings interact with variously motivated external ones. And (pre-) historic reconstruction, linguistic or otherwise, presupposes such unfoldings. I think that we can adopt the biologist's concept and term, "oriented evolution," for this interplay between the internal and the external and the related interplays between the random and the determined, the arbitrary and the nonarbitrary, in the evolution of language.

But a general theory of language change differs from theories of the biological and physical world in some profound ways that echo the profound differences between physical and linguistic relativity. There exists an interesting position that I would like to mention though I cannot affirm it. At one level, the only reality for language is the here and now; that language makes present whatever it entertains; that the past of language has survived into its present and the future of language is an anticipatory implication. In these terms, intentionally couched in an extreme form, language contains its past and future as its present or contains its time and its processes within itself. This increases the complexity of the present and hence the individuality and nontranslatability of language.

DESTRUCTION/BUILDING

> Like a piece of ice on a hot stove, a poem must ride on its own melting.
>
> ROBERT FROST, *"The Figure a Poem Makes"*

Closely related to these paradoxes of temporality is another paradox. At any time language is tending to lose its cohesion and structure, to disintegrate, with bits and pieces flying off into disuse, relative randomness, or oblivion. But while it is tempting to use the metaphor of centrifugal force for this outward flying, it seems just as true that the processes may consist of a turning inward, an increase of density, a concentration of language that is destructive. In other words, the relatively negative forces of language are both centrifugal and centripetal. These forces may be gradual; at other times their speed and comprehensiveness in the imagination or culture can reach irreparable levels of chaos—be it advanced language dying or the accelerated agrammatism of aphasia. But we must also recognize that these mainly destructive forces, whether languid or rapid, can also be sources of innovation and renovation.

The mainly destructive, centripetal and centrifugal forces in language are, in any case, balanced by equally strong tendencies to grow, to tighten or loosen as needs be, to become more integrated and synthesized. The diffuse meanings of a loaded word such as "Chicano" can be tightened and reinforced by a healthy political awareness; the inconsistencies in a set of syntactic or stylistic rules may be eliminated through analogy; and one's total knowledge and feel for a foreign language may be assured through a protracted relationship with a monolingual speaker. These obvious experiences of language building and creating cannot be treated in isolation, or we end up in a position similar to that of the historical linguists who invoke rule-simplification as an explanation while ignoring the countervailing processes of rule-complication, or the position of the cultural anthropologists who assume that the normal tendency is toward ever greater harmony and internal stability in culture.

I would assume that the processes of creation and destruction always entail an interplay between internal and external forces—like everything else in the world. In other words, language tends simultaneously to create and to destroy itself "from within" even while the externals, the environment or the ecology of language, tend simultaneously to create and destroy it from without. All four processes are taking place at the same time. It is reminiscent of the interacting (and partly random) processes of genetic mutation and the decay of genetic variability in biology. Similarly, the continuous interaction of all four processes in language might be named by the idea/word "homeostasis," taken from biology—except that this word emphasizes the static. I would prefer the term "homeodynamics" to capture the basic ingredients of constant creation and destruction.

The interacting processes of creation and destruction overlap with those of entropy, or the tendency toward structural implosion. Like many fundamental linguistic and other symbolic processes, they are illustrated most clearly by verbal art; for instance, by the song or lyric poem that "works." Such poems may almost defeat the intelligence (Stevens) or avoid saying what is meant (Frost) or teeter along the division between the grammatical and the agrammatical or even the antigrammatical (Cummings). In short, they create the illusion of randomness, entropy, or disintegration from within. But the selfsame poem, by virtue of its many echoes and allusions and adhesions within its universe of sounds and forms and meanings, will seem to be pulling itself together into itself at an increasingly rapid rate during a recitation. The combined effect of the two antithetical but aesthetically collaborating forces may leave the reader shaken, elated, or disturbed. Perhaps the best example of the collaboration of these forces in English is Blake's "Tyger," which is a particularly powerful example because *the poem itself* is about, or refers to, the processes in question. But the paradoxical double process is at work, not only in the great poems of the Western tradition, but also in many of the finest poems of the Copper Eskimo, the Trobriand Islanders, the Aztecs, and any number of primitive and archaic peoples. Such poems mirror these processes as they condense experience into a single equivalent that is felt to be maximally necessary; both achievements create a paradoxical and partly chaotic power.

THE ORDER-TO-CHAOS CONTINUUM: ORDER, REGULARITY, DETERMINACY, PREDICTABILITY, RANDOMNESS, FREEDOM, CHOICE, CHAOS

> The subject matter of poetry is not that "collection of solid static objects extended in space" but the life that is lived in the scene that it composes; and so reality is not that external scene but the life that is lived in it.
>
> WALLACE STEVENS, *The Necessary Angel*

The paradox of destruction and building leads to the deeper ones of order and chaos and points in between. Our sense of the order in language arises from our ordinary everyday experience of sounds and syntax and meaning, and is experienced at many levels. For linguists, this impression of order is bolstered by the perennial hardiness of the phoneme, the phrase, and similar units. A different kind of order is represented by tough, probabilistic, and sometimes, perhaps, exceptionless rules for the unilateral implications between rules of order. The main syntactic processes or transformations (commutation, deletion, recursive application, and so forth) and the many kinds of linear series that we find in language comprise additional universal orderings. Yet others consist of taxonomies, that is, tiers of class-inclusion relations, and the many kinds of matrices and paradigms that are governed by iconicity; for example, by the external iconicity with spatial and temporal coordinates, or the formal iconicity between two or more sets within a language (e.g., the deictic particles and the deictic verbal suffixes, or the terms for colors/directions/clans/qualities, etc. in many Amerind groups). Finally, sets may be ordered in the way they index processes in the speech situation, or the cultural ideology, or the natural world, or yet other universes. Some of the most fine-filigreed ordering has been worked out by the philologists; for example, what is known about the Greek dactylic hexameter. The multitude of types of orders should suggest the significant degree to which language is patterned and predictable.

Such specific kinds of ordering group themselves into two larger, more comprehensive ones. By the first of these, small and limited sets of rules and patterns always fall, at least in part, into larger hierarchies or similar ordered arrangements on the basis of a number of interacting dimensions. These dimensions include frequency, class inclusion, markedness, and role in contiguous hierarchies. The fundamental nature of the hierarchizing process in small and contiguous sets does not, of course, imply overall monolithic process or a totally ordered structure—as most of the leading theorists until very recently seem to have wanted. (One thinks, for example, of Whorf's imaginary "central exchange system" of language, or Chomsky's central algorithm of rules for generating all possible sentences in a language, or Lévi-Strauss's contention that his sytem of analogies is a model of the universal human mind.)

The second major and overlapping kind of order is that through which one set generates another. This may be by derivation within the morphology, as when the word "duchess" is derived from "duke" by a regular process. Another example: a set of verbal roots combines with a set of suffixes according to certain formulae and patterns of usage to yield tens of thousands of "long words" in an American Indian language. The syntactic processes of commutation and the like (combined with rules of intonation) yield a potentially infinite number of actual sentences and, in languages such as English, are more powerful and salient than morphological derivation. Depending on one's model, these output sentences can be described by branching tree diagrams, taxonomies, and/or rewrite rules. Deeper and vaguer levels of ordering have been explored for oral poetry, where generic patterns for classes of formulae serve as models for creation by analogy. Other types of derivation (most of them not understood) enable one to convert from one scientific nomenclature to another, or from one myth to another, or to condense a myth to a gist in the form of a one-sentence paradox. The two general kinds of ordering—generation/producing and hierarchizing—both illustrate the constructive or building processes in language.

To many sorts of internal and external orderings we may add several kinds of external control on their interaction. We know, for one, that language is governed partly by universals of psychology. One of these is the mind's capacity for applying rules repeatedly and, to be more inclusive, recursively—and the limitations on the number of such recursions. Of course, one finds long strings in technical discussions, such as those of anthropologists on kinship, but the reaction of the tyro to "mother's mother's brother's son" will be, "What did you say?" Conversational fluency with such coding requires practice. The apparent exceptions (e.g., alleged cases of six embeddings) only somewhat extend the outer limits in question and barely vitiate their force.

In addition to such formal constraints, language is partly determined by universals of content and of practical experience, as has been noted in chapters 3 and 5. There are thousands of cultural universals, such as ambivalence within the family and between adjoining ethnic groups. And there are many emotional universals, such as empathy, jealousy, fear, hunger, and togetherness. And there are universals of the natural world such as the biological phasings of childhood and old age (and the way they determine language learning and forgetting). Perhaps the most powerful of the universals of experience arise from the facts of the human body, with its bilateral symmetry, hand-eye coordination, organs of speech—all of which constrain the workings of the languages of the world. These factors—psychological, logical, cultural, and physiological—partly determine the structure and use of language or, more simply, partly determine what language can do and what you can or have to do with language.

The present case for a more relativistic view of order runs counter to the linguists and anthropologists who have been exaggerating the evidence and patterning discussed above. Their assumption that order is meaning and that order is the basic reality is perhaps best suggested by a list drawn from the technical terms for the object of study. These terms, to remind you, include structure, code, system, device, algorithm, rule-governed behavior, machine, computational device, set of sets, the set of rules for generating all possible sentences, and "the system of symbols and their meanings." Now, all these terms and the models to which they refer have analytical usefulness, but as uncritically used labels for grammar or the linguist's language or for culture itself, they have persistently implied a degree of order and regularity that may not correspond to anyone's experience.

The rage for order has deep intellectual-historical roots that, for many anthropologists, go back to the mechanistic rationalism of the seventeenth and eighteenth centuries and/or the mechanism-oriented spirit of the nineteenth. Linguists also get much of their orientation toward order from these sources. However, their/our profession goes back at least to the Sanskrit grammarian who, proverbially, would rather trim his grammar by one rule (i.e., make it more parsimonious) than conceive a son. That this is not only a quaint, semimythical anecdote from a patriarchal culture is suggested by the spectacle of the leading phonologists of the 1960s evaluating the economy of a phonology on the basis of whether or not it had a smaller number of "intrinsically ordered rules"—that is, thirty-six versus thirty-seven such rules.

Firm faith in a mechanistic order in language and culture has often been combined with the principle of "fruitfulness" (or heuristic value) to mislead linguists into both exaggerating order in the phenomenon being studied and generalizing it. This emerges in the statements by leading theorists that language, in this ordered sense, is ubiquitous, all-pervasive, and universally operative: a sort of projection onto the entirety of experience of a linguistic order from which no one is ever free—a claim which is of course partly, but only partly true. It also emerges in the many statements and pronouncements to the effect that language is the most powerful of human resources, that which separates us from the beasts, that which puts us in touch with the preternatural—all of which has some truth value but not the all-encompassing, religious truth that is suggested. Finally, language is often equated with knowledge or, commuting the claim, knowledge is alleged to be reducible to language: because language structure constitutes the foundations of science (Bloomfield), because scientists need to look to linguists for their perspective (Whorf), because language is equatable with all possible sentences and the device or algorithm for "generating" them (Chomsky), or because, as Wittgenstein had it, the limits of language are the limits of one's world. (Incidentally, if linguistics were going to be useful to physicists, they would have taken it into account long ago.)

The major theorists who talk in these terms assume that language *in their sense* is all-encompassing, the most fundamental reality—that language constitutes "the really real," to borrow White-head's felicitous term for the nature of God and the religious experience.

We have, in these theories, an implicit equation between language and an omnipresent, omnipotent, and omniscient force. The equation is rephrased by many anthropologists speaking about culture—particularly those who have been most influenced by linguistic models. The equating of language (or of other parts of culture) with the major force in our experience or with the most essential reality carries back, in progressively more poetic and, shall we say, enraptured form, to mythic and religious texts at least as far back as those of the Bronze Age Indo-Europeans and Semites; that is, to the Rig Veda and the Old Testament, where "the Word was God." The language of the linguistic or anthropological theorist is rooted in a personal credo that has venerable origins. These theological wellsprings suggest that linguistics and some of anthropology are humanistic in specific ways that resemble (but also differ from) those of physics and, even more, those of poetry.

Let us turn from these theologically tinged linguistic mechanisms—or rather, these irrational faiths in the total ordering of language and culture. We shall have to look critically at most descriptions and theories, whether those of psycholinguists, sociolinguists, or straight linguists (both descriptivist and transformationalist), because the extreme empiricism of the sociolinguist's mechanism and the extreme rationalism of the transformationalist's mechanism, for example, are equally absolute as they have been formulated in particular cases.

I would repeat at the outset, that a deep philosophical skepticism is most appropriate for linguists today, when we have little cause for optimism and few grounds for belief in any perfection in the world.

I would propose that language is unordered or poorly ordered to a greater extent than would be surmised from linguistic theories. It is not simply hedged about or interfered with by these lacks of order, nor can the relative lacks of order be consigned to the levels of the individual, behavior, output, pragmatics, or so on. The relative lack of order, which may verge on or merge into chaos, is an intrinsic presence that may be minor but is invariable, unavoidable, and important.

These contentions may be illustrated by introspection, something that has been much maligned recently. Purely rationalist introspection is not an adequate basis for linguistics, and no contemporary linguist has ever claimed that it was. It is just as inadequate to follow the radical empiricists and exclude any and all introspection from linguistic theory (partly because of the neurological evidence for an introspective system and its partial independence from the manipulative one of language use). I would ask you to introspect for a few moments in a general way about your own introspection. . . . Having done that I doubt you would claim that all the words and syntactic constructions crossing your imagination were the output of mechanical algorithms of some sort—as contrasted with, let us say, a sea of thoughts, feelings, images, and general perceptions. I hasten to add that ignorance and our awareness of that ignorance, as linguists, may be a component of the lack of order, but that this cannot be equated with the lack of order. It is not enough to say that we are intelligent people at the center of the unintelligible. The lack of order is also in "the data" and in the grammar, in the language "out there."

Let us move from introspection to some suggestive materials drawn from research. First, pidgin languages and jargons and similar mixtures and blends have benefited from the best analytical work of some exceptional linguists. At times, these linguists have focused on the minimal workable structures by which minimal practical and cognitive communication takes place. At other times they have partly captured less ordered, perceptual, and imagistic phenomena. Such less ordered language typically includes jumbled vocabularies, the partly haphazard interweaving of the source languages, and low predictability. It is describable, in part statistically, in part through histories and tape recordings. It may endure for decades.

There are other examples from research, described in chapter 4. For instance, as was shown in chapter 5, a major function of language is to represent, mediate, mirror, or otherwise relate to the unconscious as it surfaces in dreams, lapses of memory, and other partly chaotic images and impulses. Again, as already noted, social turbulence may lead to decreasing orderliness in a sound system; for example, in my own research, the extraordinary phonological heterogeneity, at times chaotic, in San José Tarascan was largely sidestepped—apart from a treatment of the externals—in favor of the more consistent and "legitimate" system of an "ideal informant" from one of the conservative, more endogamous, and phonologically stable villages. Finally, we note that any "fifty-fifty rule" is largely unconnected with determining contexts: the choice between "shall" and "will" or "that" and "which" for some speakers.

Let us move from anecdotes to more systematic arguments. To

begin with, one of the most powerful facts about language is its totality, its gestalt-in-process. At any time, one can select a thin part of
language—the morphology of the English verb, say, or the reference
of English kinship terms—and analyze it to a degree that may seem
complete, even penetrating. Today, however, the statements on these
subjects made in the 1950s and the 1960s do not seem particularly
"courageous" and have come to constitute significant but only small
components or background for current analysis. Since even minute
subsystems are understood so defectively at any given time, where
does this leave the astronomical complexity of the relations between
thousands of rules, features, and processes?

The so-called non-uniqueness of the linguist's solutions to language structures was originally and timelessly formulated by Chao
with particular reference to phonetics/phonemics in Chinese, but
his argument holds as well for today's generative phonology and, indeed, for any linguistics of any language. Concomitant with non-
uniqueness, the beautiful solutions in linguistics retain a high valid-
ity over time: there is no decrease in truth value as we go back, in
phonology, from Halle to Bloomfield to Saussure to Panini; the same
could be said for many truth values in ethnography. Of course, there
has been a natural-science sort of growth in parts of these fields, even
more in syntax and in natural-science-related subfields such as phonetics and neurolinguistics. But the perennial non-uniqueness of
descriptions implies a lack of order within the systems or, more
precisely, in the relation between the linguist-anthropologist and
what he/she is describing. This non-uniqueness is different from and
should not be confused with Bohr's precise "principle of complemen-
tarity" in physics by which, for example, the phenomenon of light is
recognized as both waves and particles. It is, however, similar to
Heisenberg's "principle of indeterminacy" (which partly inspired it).

A statement about language is always a statement about (the
mind of) a linguist or at least a person contemplating language; the
same can be said concerning statements about culture. The linguist,
because of the comparatively mathematical structure of language,
may achieve the sort of perennial truthfulness already noted—as in
Verner's Law or in the beautiful equations scattered through the
pages of Benveniste, which I find analogous to the truthfulness of
Pythagoras's Theorem or Euler's Theorem. But because language also
has a second, poetic dimension, another kind of perennial truthfulness may be achieved through the vivid and elegant description
of highly concrete "data"—consider such *tours de force* as Jones's
phonetics of British or Laughlin's lexicography of Mayan. These

and other apprehensions and equations may indeed give intimations of perfection. But the same partly poetic and partly mathematical truths and their combinations are exceptions rather than the rule. "Grammars leak," as Sapir put it—both the linguists' descriptions and the language "out there." This is one way of affirming, not "analytic despair," but some of the substance of the non-uniqueness that was discussed above.

The problem of perfection in language—if a digression is permitted—also is raised by poetry. Some poems may be close to perfect—one thinks of our great semipagans, Whitman and Frost, and of hundreds of individual poets who were fated to write "one perfect poem." As in the case of linguistics, the possible perfection of these poems does not depend on symmetry; on the contrary, all of them are to some extent asymmetrical or off center. It does depend, on the contrary, on such frankly arational criteria as "full realization" or the practical impossibility of changing "a single syllable." A stronger case can be made for some works of Bach and Mozart, which are not only "realized" but are perfect in an explicit, mathematically formulable sense (without, be it noted, perpetuating "a violent disorder"). Aside from these possible exceptions, however, the overwhelming majority of poems and works of music are incompletely realized and also, in some sense, imperfectly ordered.

Let us turn to the incomprehensible vastness of language. This vastness is shown, in part, by the way "language" runs by diverse rules. The workings of morphophonemics and the workings of the presuppositions and arguments of, for instance, a political rhetoric are markedly different from each other, and what they share is mediated by other subsystems. The disjunctions between the subsystems of language correspond to the differential workings within these subsystems of such basic logical processes as negation, class inclusion, degree of internal contradiction, and less logical processes such as degree of redundancy and degree of formal symmetry. These and other differentials are reflected and projected by the proliferation of language-study subfields and by the oft-lamented fact that the various practitioners feel that they can work in ignorance of each other's research. Think of the mutual indifference of phoneticians and language philosophers, or poeticians and neurologists—despite the relevance of each of these fields for the others. None of the dozens of recent articles on word order takes into account the neurological probability that surface word order is controlled by Wernicke's region in the brain. The proliferation of subfields also raises the heretical speculation that "language" (like "culture") is an obsolete folk category, no more appropriate as a "field of inquiry" than is "nature."

The multiplicity of linguistic modes and data and their mathematics indicates that a major theoretical enterprise for the future will be the elaboration, not of one all-encompassing scheme such as the monolithically oriented linguists aspire to, but of models and matrices that interrelate different subsets of the total. This would seem to parallel recent physics in which one great design has become a lost illusion to most theorists, who now recognize at least three great subuniverses run by irreconcilable rules, only some of which may be linked by linking theories. In linguistics, such linking or mediating theories will differ formally from intersystemic and inter-intersystemic theories. They will naturally tend to generate inter-intersystemic models that will increase our understanding of order and our intuition of the chaos interspersed within it and lying beyond it. Nonetheless, one must approve the efforts of those who have been trying to elaborate a theory of communication and culture that could include the ideas of economics, biology, linguistics, music, anthropology, and various other subsets of relevant fields.

The fact of linguistic pluralism is just one of the more systematic arguments that order is limited. Another argument is that the metalinguistic and language-using capacities of any one imagination or culture are disturbed by the fact that language itself is constantly changing, and that both its growth and its decay are significantly beyond full, rational, mechanistic control or even understanding, both at the peripheries and through the central areas. Constant flux implies some chaos. "The squirming facts exceed the squamous mind."

Linguistics, like poetry, selects and imposes an order on language elements that is beyond ordinary experience. The rigor and elegance of phonology or of an ethnoscientific statement may create a disorder or intensity or concentration that is somehow analogous to the workings of the centripetal forces of language discussed above: "a violent order is a disorder." I have felt the violence of this disorder in many a "componential analysis" and in structuralist reworkings of other phonologists' phonologies.

Language, as has been emphasized, is always significantly a matter of the unique individual. It follows that linguistic and anthropological theory must take full cognizance of both the native speaker and the analyzer, the participant-observer. Whether as analyst or as native, the individual's language is always to a significant degree linear, hierarchizing, discrete, digital, and algorithmic to some extent, but it is also just as significantly diffuse, metaphoric, appositional, and open-ended (for neurological as well as anthropological reasons). It follows that the language-using imagination, *as an analytical construct*, must be conceptualized as having both an ordered and a less ordered, partly chaotic dimension. Since this language-using imagination is necessarily connected with "language," it follows that our idea of language, especially of grammar, must include and entertain a significant degree of disorder, chaotic freedom, free play, and the like.

Aside from these individualistic arguments for a component of chaos, there is the problem of Gödel's principle: any formal system— and any language, for grammar is to a degree a formal system—can predicate or generate propositions that contravene its usual output or implications. Contrary to a perhaps prevailing opinion, I feel that linguistics is "ready" for Gödel's principle.

The lack of order may be formal, granted that the formal/substantive dichotomy, also a matter of degree, has all too often been exaggerated. There may be low iconicity between the reference of a sentence and a set of spatial or temporal coordinates. Or there may be low congruence between the spatiotemporal coordinates in some subsystem, such as the tense and aspect subsystem, and the spatiotemporal coordinates in some larger sense—whether these be projections of language or the formal implications of culture in some more inclusive meaning. Formal lack of order includes the probably typical case of a paradigm that lacks a member or a linear series that lacks a number. The relative lack of order may involve small groups of rules or symbols, but tends to be greater the more we move into relations between large groups and sets.

Lack of order, from the analyst's point of view in particular, may also refer to the enormous generative power of transformations in syntax and in similar derivational processes—a power that, at first inebriating to many linguists and then disillusioning, led some individuals to reject transformations altogether or to be further confirmed in their original rejection. Others reverted to "Cartesian rationalism" and an adventure in setting back the theoretical clock by three centuries. Others went to the extreme of envisaging language as a sort of cage without walls (e.g., the idea that grammar is only a "system of constraints" or that meaning is only "by contrast").

On the other hand, many people outside of or peripheral to linguistics felt and feel that the supposedly excessive power of the transformations developed by Chomsky and others implies something profoundly true about the nature of language. They have experienced the connection between these "wild" transformations and the yet more powerful and comprehensive process of analogy. They have seen that, through analogical processes, the language-using imagination, notably in children, makes untold new contributions to the life of language—some of them extra, useless, deviant, and agrammatical, others highly useful, needed, and filling various niches in the language process. "Lack of order," then, refers in part to the creative potential in language and related cultural processes.

Lack of order in these more positive senses overlaps with the strong forces of creation and destruction that I introduced above: the simultaneously centrifugal and centripetal process of language loss and aphasia and the often chaotic forces of innovation, invention, and language building. Here, both positive and negative feedback are partly chaotic and can, at high levels, destroy or partly disintegrate language in the imagination or in a culture as well as create it.

Chaos also includes many kinds of emptiness or lacunae or "holes in the system," ranging from mutually contradictory rules in a phonology or syntax, to "zero lexemes" and other zero elements in the structure of the lexicon, to the sporadic avoidance of a basic theme or symbol in a mythic cycle, to certain silences in a conversation. Together with and complementary to silence, chaos also includes relatively high levels of "noise" from both within and without any language process.

Lack of order also includes the many asymmetries in some geometrical sense that are familiar to any practicing grammarian or language teacher. And it includes the various kinds of indeterminacy, arbitrariness, and nonpredictability that are found at all levels in all languages.

The concept of lack of order is comprehensive not only in these "horizontal" senses that cut across different processes but also in a partly vertical one that involves many levels of reality. Some of these are: (1) the language and/or language-using imagination of the unique individual, whether as analyst-observer or simply as a native speaker; (2) the language of the community or of the generic individual or "ideal speaker-hearer"; (3) the language of the grammarian or other linguist—a highly specialized type of analyst-observer; (4) language in relation to other codes and languagelike systems, particularly in culture but also in the biological and physical world (the genetic code, the code of physics); (5) language at a metaphenomenal level. These levels of language are not, of course, mutually exclusive; on the contrary, they overlap and imply each other, and the case for the significance of the lack of order is strengthened by the intersections.

The multiplicity of the levels of order is more than matched by the complex interweaving of the orders of language. Degrees of chaos as well as the illusion of the chaotic inform the transformations, associations, and mappings between aesthetic media; between, for instance, one or more of the following: plastic art, graphic art, the dance, poetry, music, and film. Such synaesthetic or multimedia experience is typical of song-language and poetry-language in primitive, archaic, and peasant cultures. It is also salient in the opera-ballet or in the attempts of an individual to link one form such as poetry with another such as music. But the workings of the inter-media process, even in these self-conscious, modern examples, are hardly understood—partly because the number of ways of setting a poem to music or of writing music for a poem are enormous; Stevens's "Thirteen Ways of Looking at a Blackbird" has already been set to music thirteen times and the list grows. Inter- or multimedia art or art with rich intermedia resonances is not, in any case, designed so that the associations be reducible or paraphrasable in some discursive language. The problems of intermedia mapping are compounded when we move into all the possible associative responses to the possible participants—to the musical responses in an audience at a poetry reading or the poetic responses in an audience at a symphony. The life of language here, as in multiple tracking in a conversation, is significantly random, asymmetrical, paradoxical, and chaotic.

The terms/concepts "lack of order" and "degrees of order" are preferable to such suggested alternatives as "arbitrary," "random," "indeterminate," or "unpredictable," and their positive counterparts (predictable, and so forth). "Lack of order" is more comprehensive and, in Peirce's sense, more precise in its degree of vagueness. It refers to an overriding, synthetic generalization about many of the processes in language and culture, processes that at times contradict one another. "Lack of order" is more suggestive and informative than the alternatives.

CHAOS

A. A violent order is a disorder; and
B. A great disorder is an order. These
Two things are one
  WALLACE STEVENS, *"Connoisseur of Chaos"*

And then are burst the three dimensions' bonds
And universal seas revealed.
  OSIP MANDELSTAM, *"The Pedestrian"*

The term/idea "chaos" has been used above as a more specific and positively valued subcategory of "lack of order." Chaos is connected with creation, intellectual freedom, the unique individual, and the emotional side of language and imagination. Chaos is also indispensable theoretically as the logical counterpart of order: neither is meaningful without the other; neither can be defined without the other; neither has any reality as an absolute, absolute order and absolute chaos are meaningless and nonexistent. Chaos in these diverse anthropological and linguistic senses is connected in a natural way with many or most of the colloquial and literary meanings as well as with the cosmological and mythological ones in many myths about the origin of humankind, language, and reality. We do not need these archaic mythic dimensions for the thesis being worked out here, but I think we should be aware of them.

The reality of lack of order and, even more, of chaos in language is suggested by the way *most* linguists and linguistic theorists have, in their/our rage for order, maintained a general silence on or avoidance of the entire subject. Linguists, like logicians, don't like to recognize that, as the Russian poet Tjutchev put it in a poem, "An idea once expressed is a lie." Some linguists, because of their/our affinity with logicians, have tended to take "truth values" too seriously and to neglect culturally structured patterns of mendacity, deceit, illusion, hearsay, and prejudice. The claim that the basicness of chaos is evidenced by linguists' taboo on it rests on the anthropological assumption that the basic concerns of a culture—here the culture of linguists—are often masked or implicit because to raise them would create anxiety.

Many of us have overemphasized the discreteness of units, the depth of structures, the strictness of rule ordering, freedom from context, and the linearity of messages in single-track communication, as we have static structures or at least highly ordered, sequential structures; for example, witness the metaphor that language is like a game of chess, or the typical descriptivist grammars, or the implausible strings of intrinsically ordered rules that were advocated recently. These diverse excesses are what one would expect to result from cognitive-referential models that have partly outlived their own assumptions. The transient successes of the users of these models sometimes resemble those of the orthodox Freudians, who, with their self-fulfilling beliefs in a fully determined and sexual motivation of all human acts, can always find or invent a "Freudian" explanation to get them to where they want to end up. The cognitive-referential models have, of course, been fruitful and productive to a great extent, partly because so much of language *is* logical and referential, as emphasized above. The basic goal, as I see it, is to circumspectly exploit these cognitive-referential models for what they are worth, which is usually a good deal, *without* reifying them or alienating language from experience.

Many linguists' exclusive attention to order stems from thinking only at the level of the communal, or of the generic individual, the "ideal-speaker-hearer," or of past "stages" of language—where, that is, there has been an unwillingness to define the individual and language and their mutual relation in some usable way. The more we get into language as used and known and felt by actual, concrete individuals, the more we recognize the role of chaos in the life of language.

The fallacy implicit in ignoring disorder and chaos is shown by the way students of language, contrary to experience and intuition, often confuse analytical, structural, or logical depth with psychological depth. On the one hand, for example, an analytically deep syntactic or kinship-algebraic rule may have no known meaning to the speakers of the language, and there may in fact *be* no such ascertainable meaning. On the other hand, the so-called surface phone or single word, in the form of an outcry, may symbolize the cruel trauma of an individual; a so-called surface rule of syntax may symbolize just as directly the tragic conflicts between rival Latino street gangs; a color term such as scarlet may stand for an underlying chromatic meaning—and also for nonchromatic meanings such as adultery and lust. In such cases one may assume more or less direct symbolization without much in the way of mediating structures and categories, as long as context is specified, as it always must be. In other words, such surface units relate directly to deep psychological levels, particularly in the unconscious, without being alternates or variants in a well-ordered rule system of some sort. Much of language learning and remembering and use works in this way.

The fallacy of assuming too much order also depends on our ignorance of the speed and the paths by which the language-using imagination moves between forms, sounds, meanings, and structures. Some innocent word such as yellow, for example, may trigger "California mellow" then "Jelly Roll Morton" and so on, and the mind in any one of the moves seems to take little or no time; that is, it moves instantaneously. This partial and frequent instantaneity has been obscured by artificial testing situations with all of their built-in conditioning to make the subject lag in responding. Otherwise, our tests for measuring the speed of the language process— which may be our analogue for the speed of light—are still as grossly empirical as the ones Galileo used for light in the sixteenth century. When we have a better idea of the speed of language we will understand better the relation between the relatively ordered sets of speech output and the relatively unordered knowledge of language and how information is passed back and forth between these universes.

It is philosophically absurd to deny the importance of a lack of order in language. But it would be almost as absurd to insist on ascertaining the precise amounts of the elements discussed above, beyond establishing that they are significant and may be large. The degree of implementation varies enormously between individuals, historical situations, and cultures, and in some cases can be high without greatly impairing other functions. This ability to function with poorly ordered systems seems analogous to the fact, now fairly well researched and established, that individuals can cooperate and communicate in groups without much shared understanding or cultural background.

Clearly, the uses and non-uses of chaos entail research problems that are neglected by students of language today (by "non-uses" I mean that silence, asymmetry, syntactic scrambling, and the like may have no non—ad hoc function—and that the whole idea of "use" becomes problematical once we discard any strict and consistent functionalism). Perhaps the most general of the research problems that are raised would be to show empirically that many of the orders that have been posited are actually false reductions or false expansions, or that the data that were, so to speak, overordered, were/are in fact significantly chaotic. These accomplishments, if achieved or indeed achievable, would, within the usual methodological framework, set up chaos as a strong claim rather than a speculative generalization. Such "proofs," on the other hand, would always be falsifiable or could always be explained away; and this concept of proof is itself inappropriate. All that we can ever hope to show is that language is mainly ordered and patterned in its processes but that some of what seems ordered is actually unordered (or even chaotic) and that, to a larger extent, much of what seems unordered eventually turns out to be ordered; rather than being diametrically and dialectically counterposed, order and chaos are overlapping, interacting, and mutually contextualizing. In this sense, my case for the role of lack of order, like that for the relative nonarbitrariness of the symbol, is partly metaphenomenal.

The above meditations, mainly philosophical, do not boil down to advocating that linguists start writing poems or that anthropologists limit themselves to the ethnographic film—although these and other alternatives that sound extreme are worthwhile in some contexts. What I *am* advocating is that linguists, anthropological and otherwise, expand our horizons to include more of the lack of order and even the chaotic in grammars and in cultural analyses of language. This could be done through nondiscursive views of the subject or discursive representations of chaotic phenomena. It could take the form of an analysis that sorts out some of what matters without necessarily claiming to tell how it is put together, or of describing a unique case of turbulence or revolution without claiming to capture the universal laws that govern it. Or it could represent or otherwise symbolize the chaotic and unordered in ways that communicate or suggest its meaning without necessarily reducing it to flow charts, taxonomies, diagrams, or rewrite rules.

The relatively unordered, free, or even *chaotic* sorts of reality are already dealt with by sophisticated strategies in physical anthropology, communications theory, symbolic anthropology, film, painting, poetry, music, and many other arts and sciences. These apprehensions of the reality of lacks of order range from empirical studies of noise in communication, to the statistics of genetic mutation and genetic decay, to the paintings of Jackson Pollock, to the poetry (and theories of poetry) of John Ashbery, to a recognition of the theoretical connections between chaos in language and chaos in mythology. (For example, the "male and female principles" in many systems of myth are certainly related to grammatical and mythical modes of thought.) And even in linguistics the conceptualization of a relative lack of order is not particularly speculative; it refers to published research, much of it discussed above, by the many persons who more or less intentionally have been concerned with the creation of what might be called an "open view" of language and an open linguistics.

Indeed, the present article is at one level an advocacy of just such an open linguistics.

The present case, then, is not for chaos but for chaos and other lacks of order as contrasted with the various degrees and kinds of order; in other words, a meditation on order and disorder in terms of a half dozen dimensions. The paradox of order and lack of order is the most profound and interesting in language. It may have been worthwhile to set forth its main outlines and perhaps open up some new lines of thought. A full abstract argument with full empirical exemplification would require two to four hundred pages and no doubt lead the adventurous author into a new general theory of language.

RELATIVITY

> Our interest lies, not in questions such as, "What does this form, or form class, mean?" but, instead, in the question, "In what manner does a language organize, through its structural semantic system, the world of experience in which its speakers live?"
>
> HARRY HOIJER, *"The Sapir-Whorf Hypothesis"*

Let us return to the initial and more general problem of linguistic relativity and its relation to the network of paradoxical dimensions. Recall that these dimensions are partly tools for analysis but also reflect one's personal experience of language. Second, recall that each dimension applies to experience along its entire length rather than just at the poles of what are ideal types. Even the metaphors implicit in "pole" or "binary opposition" are deceptive because the dimensions do not have any actual ends; either end of any dimension is indefinitely extendable as we become, analytically, more and more behavioral or more structural or more referential or more suggestive, and so forth.

The final dimension, the least orthodox and most basic, was not dealt with in terms of poles but in terms of degrees—of order and of chaos—and the diverse associations of these degrees with such things as paradox, randomness, ambiguity, determinacy, and freedom; as noted, absolute order is rare at best and absolute disorder in language even rarer. Also, recall that each of the dimensions intersects with the others, although the dimension of continuity and discontinuity is the most fundamental in some formal sense: it defines the shape of the others. And recall the dimensions themselves:

behavior/deep meaning, abstract/concrete, individual/communal, subjective/objective, linearity/instantaneity, destruction/creation. Other such dimensions would have to be dealt with in any full-scale treatment: synchrony/diachrony, context-sensitive, and so forth. All of these dimensions are complex and paradoxical in their realization. All of the dimensions and their interrelations contribute to a more adequate and abstract definition of the uniqueness of any one language-culture. But of all the dimensions that come into question, that of order-to-chaos contributes the most to linguistic relativity: the less ordered a language, the less transformable and translatable. In these terms, any translation is a loose approximation. The astronomical complexity of language from this point of view adds an abstract argument to the Humboldt—Boas—Sapir—Whorf—et al. hypothesis. The hypothesis, as we have seen, is deeply articulated and reticulated with the problem of freedom.

9

Toward an Improved Theory of Linguistic Relativism and Poetic Indeterminacy

The foregoing pages have sketched or at least suggested a theory of linguistic relativism and indeterminacy—particularly of underlying chaos and of the poetry that is in every speaker. Let me conclude with an additional, synoptic discussion of four issues that would require more detailed treatment in a more fully explicit formation. These issues are teleonomy, the creative individual, system-in-process, and aesthetic truth.

The first issue is that of the goals, purposes, and other "ends" of language. I assume, as do biologists and physicists concerning their objects, that language and other cultural systems tend in certain directions. This directionality has been demonstrated in detail for everything from phonological change to the history of artistic or political movements. The goal-directed cultural universes have to be seen as constantly interacting with biological, psychological, and other phenomena to create more complex universes that also are directed toward a goal or goals—even though the specifics may remain fuzzy or be inherently vague or at least have a seemingly high degree of randomness. The contrary assumption of absolutely "no end" is counterproductive in a heuristic sense, ignores the implications of all historical studies to date, and has other implications that are absurd. The phenomena of teleonomy in language and poetic language are of several logically distinct kinds, including what I would call axiomatic teleonomy or systematic determinism (partly dealt with above as a kind of order in the "order-to-chaos continuum").

In some ways the orientation of a cultural or linguistic group sharing goals is the polar opposite of uniquely individual teleonomies and is constrained and directed by different psychological factors. But in other ways it is analogous to such individual purpose and intention, whether or not the latter are conscious. In fact, the issue of teleonomy is intensified and clarified through a consideration of the poetic imagination of the individual. The tidelike "drift" that we infer at the social and cultural levels of language here becomes concentrated in a more subjective and immediate reality; all of us as individuals have a first-hand experience of linguistic teleonomy, but of the many sorts of speakers and even verbal artists and advertising script writers, it is the out-and-out poet—whether or not he/she writes it down—who most condenses the teleonomy of language as a quintessential fact of life, as part of an unusually dynamic and fragile point of view—fragile because the medium verges on disintegration or becomes the message. Of course, this is making a special claim for the poet and the poet's language. And it does seem to hark back to the stereotype of the poet waxing lyrical beneath the moon or losing sleep over the choice of a word or syllable—whether, at a key point, to use "a" or "the." But it also corresponds to a definite reality.

Analogous to the poet is the growing infant and child. The child somehow synthesizes the disparate and incomplete fragments of a linguistic experience and constructs a complex and in part uniquely personal grammar. This grammar is synthesized with a world view that to a significant degree is made anew by each speaker. The years spent in such construction evidence emotional, rational, and other mental activities that are intensely poetic—involving sound play, complex figures of speech, and various experiments—and that differ in kind and frequency from adult discourse. The small child and the poet have in common a naiveté, rejecting "attitudes of philosophic distrust"—even if in the form of exaggerated disillusionment. Child and poet are constantly putting together or trying to put together a language-cum-world view that reaches well beyond the resources of content and linguistic form directly available to them. The linguistic relativity hypothesis, then, can draw primary insight not only from poetry and poets but from the evidence of child language (including semantics) and from an integrated study of the two—as in chapter 3 above, which draws on Russian poetry and Russian child language.

I have already broached the second fundamental problem: that of the creative individual, or better, of the individual in a creative sense. A valuable negative definition of this individuality might include whatever grammar or use—or other linguistic structure and process—is not shared or social, just as, by another such negative definition, "poetry is what can't be translated." But a more positive way of putting this is that individuals synthesize the uniquely personal with the social and the shared to create their language; they relate to language and dialect as cultural resources and, through their needs, motivations, and other emotional and rational energies, mold them into a unique "idiolect," even a personal style. Every individual does have, if not *style*, then at least *a* style, granted that some styles entail more conscious and complex artistry than others. Is the designation "poet" equally apt for Abraham Lincoln and for his biographer, poet Carl Sandburg? Yes, because the linguistic forms of a leader may attain the majesty of the Gettysburg Address and because there is a constant relation between poetry, rhetoric, and ordinary conversational language. But the "yes" needs to be qualified in terms of some more dimensions of the "poetic," which brings me to the third of the general issues named above: system-in-process.

To begin with, the response of a reader or an audience to a powerful poem reflects and brings to the surface the potential intimacy that links together all the native or at least fluent speakers of *a* language, or even of *any* language, given our often strong intuitions for poetry in a foreign language. Psychological bonding through shared language is what fundamentally differentiates poetry from music, painting, and the other arts. Everyone is a fluent native speaker of some language while few—although they have eyes and ears—are practiced, expert painters, musicians, or the like. It is true that music and dance among the other arts also reach these territories of the imagination and in some ways go further because they are *not* constrained by language, but in other ways they do not go as far because they are not so implicated in linguistically connected experience. Poetry takes as its raw material a version of the language that the individual has grown up with or that—in the case of German immigrant Lisel Mueller, for example, or quadrilingual Vladimir Nabokov—has become totally identified with to the point that this language becomes a vehicle of identity and even *is* the individual in a way that chemistry or music or even linguistics never can be. That is why the excitement and illumination of poetry may resemble some of the other arts in its strength; it ranges from drunken madness to a music lover's sense of harmony, but exceeds them in its scope and its attachments to the minutiae of the unique mind.

Similarly, there is enormous variation across cultures, from our

American audiences, which often have little background or even interest, to the Eskimo or Russian audiences where almost everyone knows the poetic tradition and may, indeed, know thousands of lines by heart, even of the poems being recited at a performance by a popular bard. But a successful poem or a successful reading in any culture has similar primal emotional consequences.

Thus the poetic event requires, as a sine qua non, a unique double fusion. One is the special, almost pathological fusion or identification of the poet with the language and the poetic tradition. The other is the fusion of this identity with the linguistic sensitivities and experience of the audience. This strange duplex process of partly contradictory, dialectically struggling processes poses a challenge for anyone interested in the psychology of culture.

Let us explore these double dialectical fusions in terms of two cornerstone problems.

First, poetry succeeds only after many months and usually years of practice and experiment, trial and error, work and play with words, syllables, intonation, styles, forms, genres, languages, and traditions, and whatever selection of these constitutes the more essential formal matter for a given poet. (Exceptions such as Millay's *Renascence*, published when she was nineteen, turn out to be only apparent; she had been writing since childhood and was well read.) All the poets that I am concerned with (and this includes many unknown), even the most emotional, such as Dylan Thomas, and the most popular and accessible, such as Carl Sandburg, concur on the indispensable role of craft or technique in some sophisticated, deep, and exiguous genre; as Yeats said, "Poets of Ireland, learn your trade." A commitment to craft need not be compromised by an ability to occasionally produce final copy in a first draft nor by a reverence for "the sanctity of the first draft." Also, when we talk about craft we must distinguish between devices, rules, and tricks of the trade, as an inventory of means, and the psychological integration of these things with more deeply rooted intentions and designs. The linguistic relativism hypothesis of the future would deal with the poet as partly a craftsperson and partly a shaman—as are primitive and ancient poets as well as modern masters such as Lorca and Neruda and some younger poets of America today, such as Forché. I realize, incidentally, the terminological perils of this comprehensive use of the word "shaman," by which jaded and/or erudite California is sometimes grouped with the pristine vigor, so to speak, of the inspired Eskimo; I know no better term, however, to convey the senses of inspiration, primacy, deep reverberations, and the like that are involved in writing or responding to a good poem. The shaman-cum-craftsman model integrates the cognitive and the affective, the compositional and the performative, the primitive and the literary dimensions of language.

The conjunction of craftsman and shaman, of the uniquely personal and the intimately communal aspects of a poem, also underlies some of the paradoxes of its power. Admittedly, the power of the poetic word may simply be that of persuasiveness ("the pen is mightier than the sword"). But the poet tends to stand outside the institutionalized power structure (albeit not in Iceland, India, and other cultures where poetic aptitudes are essential for leadership). The comparative independence of poets and their relative freedom to attack, challenge, or simply avoid the economic and political status quo may make them dangerous, or at least seem so. As Mandelstam put it, we must be powerful or they wouldn't try to silence us; a political culture where poets are not silenced no matter what they say speaks for itself. Some awareness of the interrelations between poetry and power is necessary—rather, a corrective—to contemporary systems of poetics that tend toward a pure aestheticism or subjectivism concerned with technique, the poetry of poetry, expressiveness, surface language, and so forth. On the other hand, it is also necessary to avoid a restrictive focus on economic context and political power that converts the poet into a pawn and the poems into objects. A whole range of theoretical bridges needs to be built between these alternative views of the poem, that is, between formalism and the subjectivism with which it is associated, on the one hand, and, on the other hand, political realism, activism, and similar orientations. We need a theory that can handle Woody Guthrie's songs such as "This Land Is Your Land" or "Deportee," with their blend of lyricism and political commitment.

This brings me to the second cornerstone problem: the fact that, to begin with, our use of a term like "structure" is a practical compromise with natural language, here English. Actually, we have to think of "form" and "structure" as *nomina confusa*, as the biologists would say, involving definitions that partly contradict and partly overlap with each other. It is not that structure is an extension of content, or that one is a transformation or extension of the other. On the contrary, the two must be distinguished and are meaningless without each other; concretely, for example, the limerick form necessarily implies and excludes certain semantic content. A theory of linguistic relativism, if it is to be realistic and contemporary, must be conceptualized at once vaguely and precisely so that it transcends the partly terminological paradoxes and dilemmas of structure/content, structure/process, structure/variation, and, for that matter, subjective/objective and rational/irrational.

This having been said, what are the essential dimensions of poetry as part of a language and culture? Let me take one example. The *line* is surely one of the minimal criteria for what makes a poem, for separating poetry from prose, and for evaluating the quality of poems. But whether we define it in terms of syllable counts, of the width of a page, as a breath group, or by some other formal measure, the line (particularly in great poems) is just as much a unit that fuses meaning and form into a unit with its own centering of energy. This energy of the line, or line-energy, is part of a style and genre within an individual or collective tradition that carries with it all kinds of emotional and even ideological expectations. Linguistic relativism entertains these complex interlacings between form and content all through the poetic language process.

The idea of structure or form is also inseparable from that of variation, and neither can be subsumed under the other in a logical sense. One level of variation is the text, and we have to assume that there are as many texts as there are readings—although not, as Frost said, that a poem deserves all its interpretations. The problem of variants, so acute in the study of myth, is vastly greater in the study of poetry, since the latter includes mythic patterning as well as questions of surface form and the music of language. Ultimately the issue of variation becomes one of multiple contextualization, since any text is related to others along the axes of space, time, message, author, performance, audience or reader, the linguistic code, cultural context, and other variables in the overall life of the poem. The empirical fact of variation and the interconnectedness of variants and contexts forces us to take a consistently relativistic attitude toward poetic language and renders vacuous many absolutist claims or theoretical positions—for example, that a poem can "stand alone" or that every poet is "writing one poem."

The fourth and perhaps most basic issue to be faced by the linguistic relativism hypothesis involves our location in a gray, liminal area between art and science; between, that is, the associative, emotional, evocative values of art and, on the other hand, the values of internal consistency, "realism," and verifiability that characterize science. Poeticians who, on the ground of various misconceptions, try to equate themselves with theoretical physicists and the like have been reading "physics for poets" popularizations and ignoring how physicists construct and empirically test their theories as well as the fact that they use calculus (or some other mathematics) as their basic language, the language of conceptualization. In a similar way, intellectual historians and art critics who dwell exclusively on the philosophy and ideology of poetry ignore how poets engender poems and the vast body of technique and craftsmanship that underlies practically all poetry worthy of the name. Let us explicitly disassociate ourselves from the antiscience and radical antirationalist positions (the two are often confused). The science and mathematics of Descartes, for example, are beautiful, as is all first-rate science and mathematics, and Descartes, like his fellow scientist and mathematician Pascal, remains one of the great stylists of the French language with its peculiarly demanding traditions. Our problem is to constructively interrelate science and poetry in a new poetics.

The problematic interface between art and science that is posed or, rather, incarnated by the linguistic relativism hypothesis can be seen as a dialectical middle ground between two cogent positions. One—that of the realist—is that language is a way of describing and dealing with the outer and inner worlds, that language is *of* and *for* the world in the sense of practical problems, scientific analysis, some sort of real world "out there" in the hills and stars and "in there" within the psyche. This "real world" position is illustrated not only by scientific formulae in natural language, such as "sodium chloride," but also by such phrases as "Pass the salt," which we used as an example back in chapter 3; most speakers take it as essentially realistic, referring to a simple action and a simple object. But the realist position is also illustrated by mathematical poems—where a mathematical object is the basis of a conceit—and by highly descriptive poems in the Imagist and Objectivist traditions of red wheelbarrows that are first and foremost red wheelbarrows. Nevertheless, no poem can be purely realistic or referential for the obvious reason that "sodium chloride"—even in a chemistry lab—necessarily has all sorts of secondary connotations.

Counterposed to the "real world" position we find the more mentalistic one that language has few necessary connections with the practical or scientific world, that it pursues a more or less autonomous life. Clearly, a primal cry or a concrete word may seem inevitable after you've barked your shin, but the main reality of grammar and the more interesting parts of semantics is thought to be their independence in constituting what amounts to a world vision. The world vision theory is illustrated by the sound poems that have practically no reference aside from what may be suggested by a euphonic flow of syllables. But it is also illustrated by the above-mentioned command to "Pass the salt," which may involve anything from blanket-tossing an old sailor to walking past Lot's wife without looking. Some of the best examples of poetry liberated from reality and the usual truth values come from the great surrealists, others come from Futurism and Language poetry, and yet others arise from the fashionable position that language is based on the need for mendacity, that it is the most fundamental way of giving form to illusions. On the other hand, no world vision poem, no matter how unrealistic or surrealistic or how strongly based on sound play or how wickedly mendacious, is ever going to escape from the real world and its problems of reasonably accurate, consistent reference. Because words, idioms, and even syllables have minimal—if always probabilistic and usually fuzzy-edged—meaning for the poet and the audience.

Both world views can be realized in a single poem; for example, the fine poem "Stinging Nettle" by Gwen Head is both about its own language and about the minimal natural-historical knowledge of this weed that we would find in a good handbook; many bird poems are like this. Interstitial science-cum-art poems illuminate the interface between anthropology and poetry more than do poems that select a few symbols from an alien culture (often known second-hand) in order to construct a highly personal and specifically ethnocentric poem that might well have been written by a peripatetic poet, a desultory reader of ethnographies. The two world views can also be reconciled through a poetic ethnography that communicates the poetic dimensions in a language and culture.

The linguistic relativism hypothesis will ultimately have to build an elaborate theoretical compromise between the "world vision" position and the "real world" position, because both give us insight and both are based solidly on what we know about culture, language, psychology, poetics, and even ordinary experience. Neither is totally valid, neither works alone. The two positions can only be resolved by a concept of truth that is centered on the aesthetic, on scientific beauty and artistic beauty. "Beauty" in this sense will help us avoid the dogmatisms of realism and materialism and also of aestheticism and subjectivism. That is why the value of beauty and the idea of aesthetic form, which I advanced at the outset, remain as the vague but fundamental presence in my thought and the keystone of this book.

Notes

Chapter 5. The Poetry of Language in the Politics of Dreams

1. The Great Blue Heron (unlike the Little Green) is to a significant extent an American national, that is, pan-cultural, symbol; most Americans have seen it or at least read about it—a vague, ghostly, long-legged, greyish bird starting up out of a pond or swamp.

2. Sharon's first name, "Ariel," could in principle be connected with the archangel and (interpreting) link a positive power symbol to a negative one by what I call "the perversion commutation" of many political dreams. But, mainly because of my lack of awareness of the angel and its attributes, I doubt that this symbolic identification played a role in my dream. The peculiar spelling of "Sharonne" has been retained as it took shape when recalling the dream.

Sharon (O'Rourke) was the name of an Irish-American girl with whom I talked all night during a trans-Atlantic crossing—only to have her met by her lover in Luxembourg! This experience seems to have blocked my connecting the two Sharons until long after this article was essentially completed.

3. The way these atoms are ordered in dreams resembles a Russian folk tale à la Propp at one level and, at another, the "atomic predicates" in an old-fashioned transformational grammar. I take this, provisionally, to reflect my background as much as it describes the structure of the dream.

4. A problem that I can do no more than broach here is the relation of dream (analysis) to anthropological fieldwork and similar ostensibly empirical enterprises. The dreams of such a fieldworker are part of his/her processing "data" and even of constructing a new reality in the form of an ethnography. The way dreams are ignored by most fieldworkers suggests a deep

lack of sensitivity to or even an anxiety about the dialogic relation between the ethnographer and the culture.

Chapter 6. The Unheralded Revolution in the Sonnet: Toward a Generative Model

1. Sonnets have been written in Modern Indonesian and, to a much greater degree, in all the major East Indian languages but have remained a minor, ancillary tradition. The notable exception is Bengali, where, starting in the early nineteenth century and continuing recently in the poetry of Jibanananda Das and others, sonnets have constituted a major tradition (some of these sonneteers mastering not only English and French, but Petrarch in the original). The sonnet has been a significant genre in Modern Chinese and, at least in one case, emerged as a primary form for a major Formalist poet, Feng Chih (1905–), who, incidentally, in some sense fused the world view of Wang Wei with the form of Rainer Maria Rilke, whom he had studied in Germany.

2. Wyatt's poem, since dubbed "The Hind," actually was numbered VII in the Edgerton Manuscript and is an imitation of Petrarch's *Rime* 151; diamonds are a Petrarchan symbol of chastity. Otherwise, *noli me tangere*, "Don't touch me," was said by Christ to Mary Magdalene. The sonnet is believed to be devoted to Ann Boleyn, once Wyatt's lover, and the "Caesar" here is Boleyn's eventual husband, Henry VIII.

Bibliography

(This bibliography contains a small number of obviously [or at least apparently] relevant items that were published or brought to my attention after *The Language Parallax* was in production; they have been included for the benefit of the interested reader.)

Allen, Donald M., and Warren Tallman, eds.
    1973 *The Poetics of the New American Poetry*. New York: Grove. (See especially the statements by Duncan, Fenollosa, Olson, Snyder, and Whitman.)

Allen, Maury
    1975 *Where Have You Gone, Joe DiMaggio? The Story of America's Last Hero*. New York: Dutton.

Aristotle
    1982 *The Poetics. "Longinus" on the Sublime. Demetrius on Style*. Cambridge: Loeb Classical Library.

Attinasi, John J.
    n.d. Field notes on the Comachuen dialect.

Bakhtin, M. M.
    1981 *The Dialogic Imagination: Four Essays*. Edited by Michael Holquist; translated by Caryl Emerson and Michael Holquist. Austin: University of Texas Press.

Basso, Keith, and Henry Selby
    1976 *Meaning in Anthropology*. Santa Fe: School of American Research.

Bateson, Gregory
    1976 *Steps to an Ecology of Mind*. New York: Ballantine.

Baugh, John, and Joel Sherzer, eds.
    1984 *Language in Use: Readings in Sociolinguistics*. Englewood Cliffs, N.J.: Prentice-Hall. (See especially articles by Goffman, Gumperz, Baumann, and Paulston.)

Baumann, Richard
    1977 "Linguistics, Anthropology, and Verbal Art: Toward a Unified Perspective, with a Special Discussion of Child's Folklore." In Saville-Troike, ed., 1977:13–36.
Baumann, Richard, and Joel Sherzer, eds.
    1974 *Explorations in the Ethnography of Speaking*. Cambridge: Cambridge University Press. (See especially articles by Sherzer, Foster, Irvine, and Gossen.)
Beck, Brenda F.
    1978 "The Metaphor as Mediator between Semantic and Analogic Thought." *Current Anthropology* 19(1):83–97.
Becker, Alton L., and Aram Yengoyan
    1979 *The Imagination of Reality*. Norwood, N.J.: Ablex.
Benveniste, Emile
    1966 *Problèmes de lingüistique générale*. Paris: Gallimard.
Berlin, Brent
    1968 *Tzeltal Numeral Classifiers: A Study in Ethnographic Semantics*. The Hague: Mouton.
Berlin, Brent, and Paul Kay
    1969 *Basic Color Terms: Their Universality and Evaluation*. Berkeley and Los Angeles: University of California Press.
Black Elk
    1981 *Black Elk Speaks: Being the Life Story of a Holy Man of the Oglalla Sioux*. As told through John G. Niehardt. Lincoln: University of Nebraska Press.
Bloom, Harold
    1973 *The Anxiety of Influence: A Theory of Poetry*. New York: Oxford University Press.
Bloom, Harold, and Lionel Trilling
    1973 *Romantic Poetry and Prose*. Oxford: Oxford University Press. (See especially the sections on Coleridge and Wordsworth.)
Bloomfield, Leonard
    1926 "A Set of Postulates for the Science of Language." *Language* 2:153–64.
    1933 *Language*. New York: Holt.
Bly, Robert
    1973 "Wandering Breezes: 8." In *Li Po and Tu Fu*, edited by A. Cooper, p. 205. New York: Penguin.
    1974 "The Teeth-Mother." In *Sleepers Joining Hands*. New York: Harper and Row.
Boas, Franz
    1911 *Introduction to the Handbook of American Indian Languages*. Washington: Georgetown University Press Reprint (n.d.).
Bohr, Niels
    1958 *Atomic Physics and Human Knowledge*. New York: John Wiley and Sons.

Bright, William O.
 1976 *Variation and Change in Language: Essays by William Bright.*
 Selected and introduced by Anwar S. Dil. Stanford: Stanford
 University Press.
Brown, H. Rap
 1972 "Street Talk." In Kochman, ed., 1972 : 205 – 9.
Brown, Norman O.
 1968 *Love's Body.* New York: Random House.
Brown, Roger, and Eric Lenneberg
 1954 "A Study of Language and Cognition." *Journal of Abnormal and
 Social Psychology 49 : 454 – 62.*
Burke, Kenneth
 1973 *The Philosophy of Literary Form.* Berkeley: University of Cali-
 fornia Press. (See especially "Semantic and Poetic Meanings"
 and "On Musicality in Verse.")
Burling, Robbins
 1964 "Cognition and Componential Analysis: God's Truth or Hocus-
 Pocus?" *American Anthropologist 66 : 20 – 28.*
 1970 *Man's Many Voices.* New York: Holt, Rinehart and Winston.
Camus, Albert
 1955 *The Myth of Sisyphus and Other Essays.* Translated by Justin
 O'Brien. New York: Random House, Vintage Books.
 1956 *The Rebel: An Essay on Man in Revolt.* Translated by Anthony
 Bower. New York: Alfred A. Knopf, Vintage Books.
Capra, Fritjof
 1977 *The Tao of Physics.* New York: Bantam.
Carnap, Rudolf
 1933 *Philosophy and Logical Syntax.* London: Orthological Institute.
Carruth, Hayden
 1971 *The Voice That Is Great within Us: American Poetry of the
 Twentieth Century.* New York: Bantam.
Casagrande, Joseph
 1960 *In the Company of Man.* New York: Harper and Row.
Casagrande, Joseph, and Kenneth Hale
 1967 "Semantic Relations in Papago Folk Definitions." In *Studies in
 Southwestern Linguistics,* edited by Dell Hymes and William
 Biddle. The Hague: Mouton.
Cassirer, Ernst
 1946 *Language and Myth.* Translated by Suzanne K. Langer. New
 York: Dover.
Chao, Yuen-Ren
 1934 "The Non-uniqueness of Phonemic Solutions of Phonetic Sys-
 tems." In Joos, ed., 1957 : 38 – 55.
 1968 *Language and Symbolic Systems.* Cambridge: Cambridge University Press.

Chomsky, Noam
   1957 *Syntactic Structures.* The Hague: Mouton.
   1966 *Cartesian Linguistics.* New York: Harper and Row.
   1972 *Language and Mind.* New York: Harcourt, Brace, Jovanovich.
Chukovskij, Kornej
   1960 *Ot dvukh do pjati.* Moskow: Sovetskij Pisatel'.
Coffin, Tristram
   1961 *Indian Tales of North America: An Anthology for the Adult
          Reader.* Philadelphia: American Folklore Society.
Coleridge, Samuel T.
   1973 *Biographia Literaria* and *Organic Form.* In Bloom and Trilling
          1973:633–56.
Comrie, Bernard
   1981 *Language Universals and Linguistic Typology: Syntax and
          Morphology.* Chicago: University of Chicago Press.
Conklin, Harold
   1955 "Hanunóo color categories." *Southwestern Journal of Anthro-
          pology* 11:339–44.
   1960 "Maling, a Hanunóo Girl from the Philippines." In Casagrande
          1960:102–18.
Croce, Benedetto
   1978 *Aesthetic as Science of Expression and General Linguistic.*
          Translated by Douglas Ainslie. Boston: Nonpareil.
Culler, Jonathan
   1975 *Structuralist Poetics: Structuralism, Linguistics, and the Study
          of Literature.* Ithaca: Cornell University Press.
Derrida, Jacques
   1982 *Of Grammatology.* Translated by Gayatri Chakravorty Spivak.
          Baltimore: Johns Hopkins University Press.
DiMaggio, Joseph
   1946 *Lucky to Be a Yankee.* Introduction by James Farley; foreword
          by Grantland Rice. New York: R. Field.
Dingwall, William Orr, and Harry A. Whitaker
   1974 "Neurolinguistics." In *Annual Review of Anthropology,* edited
          by Bernard J. Siegel, pp. 301–23. Palo Alto: Annual Re-
          views, Inc.
Dixon, R. M. W.
   1974 "A Method of Semantic Description." In *Semantics,* edited by
          Danny D. Steinberg and Leon A. Jakobovits. Cambridge: Cam-
          bridge University Press.
Dobzhansky, Theodosius, and Olga Pavlovska
   1957 "An Experimental Study of Interaction between Genetic Drift
          and Natural Selection." *Evolution,* 11(3):311–19.
   1970 *Genetics and the Evolutionary Process.* New York: Columbia
          University Press.

Dolgin, Janet, David S. Kemnitzer, and David M. Scheider, eds.
  1977 *Symbolic Anthropology: A Reader in the Study of Symbols and Meanings*. New York: Columbia University Press.
Donoghue, Dennis
  1984 *Connoisseurs of Chaos: Ideas of Order in Modern American Poetry*. New York: Columbia University Press.
Dorian, Nancy
  1981 *Language Death: The Life Cycle of a Scottish Gaelic Dialect*. Philadelphia: University of Pennsylvania Press.
Duncan, Robert
  1973 "Four Selections." In Allen and Tallman, eds., 1973 : 185–206.
Edmonson, Munro
  1971 *The Book of Counsel: The Popol Vuh of the Quiche Maya of Guatemala*. New Orleans: Middle American Research Institute, Tulane University.
Eiseley, Loren C.
  1957 *The Immense Journey*. New York: Random House.
  1973 *The Innocent Assassins*. New York: Charles Scribner's Sons.
Eliade, Mircea
  1976 *Myths, Rites, Symbols*. Edited by W. C. Beane and W. G. Doty. 2 vols. New York: Harper and Row, Collophone.
Eliot, Thomas S.
  1961 "The Music of Poetry." In *The Partisan Review Anthology*, edited by W. Philips and P. Rahv. New York: Holt.
  1975 "Tradition and the Individual Talent." In *Selected Prose of T. S. Eliot*, edited by Frank Kermode, pp. 37–45. New York: Farrar, Strauss and Giroux.
Ellmann, Richard, and Robert O'Clair, eds.
  1973 *The Norton Anthology of Modern Poetry*. New York: W. W. Norton.
Emerson, Ralph Waldo
  1940 *The Complete Essays and Other Writings of Ralph Waldo Emerson*. Edited by Brooks Atkinson. New York: Modern Library. (See especially "Nature," "The American Scholar," and "The Poet.")
Faas, Ekbert
  1978 *Towards a New American Poetics: Essays and Interviews*. Santa Barbara: Black Sparrow.
Feld, Steven
  1982 *Sound and Sentiment: Birds, Weeping, Poetics, and Song in Kaluli Expression*. Philadelphia: University of Pennsylvania Press.
Fernandez, James W.
  1982 *Bwiti: An Ethnography of the Religious Imagination in Africa*. Princeton: Princeton University Press.

Finnegan, Ruth
   1977   *Oral Poetry: Its Nature, Significance, and Social Context.* Cambridge: Cambridge University Press.
Fishman, Joshua
   1960   "A Systematization of the Whorfian Hypothesis." *Behavioral Science* 9 : 323–39.
Fonágy, Ivan
   1965   "Form and Function in Poetic Language." *Diogenes* 51 : 72–110.
Foster, Mary L.
   1969   *The Tarascan Language.* University of California Publications in Linguistics, No. 56. Berkeley and Los Angeles: University of California Press.
Foster, Michael
   1974   *From the Earth to Beyond the Sky.* Ottawa: Canadian Ethnology Service Paper 20.
Frankenburg, Lloyd
   1956   *Invitation to Poetry.* New York: Doubleday.
Freud, Sigmund
   1954   *A General Introduction to Psychoanalysis.* Garden City, N.Y.: Doubleday Permabooks.
   1950   *The Interpretation of Dreams.* Translated by James Strachey. New York: Basic Books.
Friedrich, Carl J.
   1942   *The New Belief in the Common Man.* New York: W. W. Norton.
Friedrich, Paul
   1971   *The Tarascan Suffixes of Locative Space: Meaning and Morphotactics.* Bloomington: University of Indiana Press.
   1974   *On Aspect Theory and Homeric Aspect.* Memoir 28, *International Journal of American Linguistics.*
   1975   *A Phonology of Tarascan.* Chicago: University of Chicago, Department of Anthropology.
   1977   *Agrarian Revolt in a Mexican Village.* Chicago: University of Chicago Press.
   1978   *The Meaning of Aphrodite.* Chicago: University of Chicago Press.
   1979   *Language, Context, and the Imagination: Essays by Paul Friedrich.* Stanford: Stanford University Press.
   1980   Review of *Studies in the Kinship Terminology of the Indo-European Languages, with Special Reference to Indian, Iranian, Greek, and Latin*, by Oswald Szemerenyi. *Language* 56(1) : 186–192.
   1984   "Tarascan: From Meaning to Sound." In *Supplement to the Handbook of Middle American Indians,* edited by Victoria Reifler Bricker, vol. 2, *Linguistics,* edited by Munro S. Edmonson, pp. 56–83. Austin: University of Texas Press.
———. (poems)

1979   *Bastard Moons.* Chicago: Waite Press. (Contains "Sketches for
       an Ode to 'The Yankee Clipper,'" pp. 42–48, and "Kinship Al-
       pha: Proto-Indo-European," pp. 74–78. "Kinship Alpha" trans-
       lated by Werner Peterman as "Verwandschaftsalpha," *Trickster*
       12–13 [1985].)
1982   "World Listener." *Redwing* (nonpaginated). Chicago: Waite
       Press.
1983–84a   "Tarascan Corn." *Aura* 17:36.
1983–84b   "Spinoza, I Love You." *The Beloit Poetry Journal* 34(3):21.
       (Reprinted in the 1985 *Anthology of Verse and Yearbook of Po-
       etry*, ed. Alan F. Pater. Beverly Hills: Monitor.)
1984a   "Tarascan Pots." *Mississippi Valley Review* 14(1):54.
1984b   "I thought I saw some Eskimos." *Poem* 52:5.
1984c   "Industrial Accident: Mexico." *Poem* 52:6.
1985a   "First Draft." *Dreamworks* 4(4).
1985b   "I wanted to pass . . ." *Wind Literary Journal* 53:11–12.
1985c   "The Master of Words." *Great River Review* 6(1):149–150.
1985d   "Elegy for Osip Mandelstam." *Images* 10(3):5.
In press b   "Generation." *Kansas Quarterly.*
Frost, Robert
1964   *Selected Letters of Robert Frost.* Edited by Lawrence
       Thompson. New York: Holt, Rinehart and Winston.
1965   "Sentence Sounds" and "The Figure a Poem Makes." In Scully
       1965:51–54, 55–58.
1966   *Selected Prose of Robert Frost*, edited by Hyde Cox and Edward
       Connery Lathem. New York: Holt, Rinehart and Winston.
1974   *The Poetry of Robert Frost.* Edited by Edward Connery Lathem.
       New York: Holt, Rinehart and Winston.
Fussell, Paul
1978   "Free Verse." *Antaeus* 30/31: *Poetry and Poetics*, pp. 296–308.
Garvin, Paul, ed.
1964   *A Prague School Reader on Aesthetics, Literary Structure, and
       Style.* Georgetown: Georgetown University Press.
Geertz, Clifford
1973   *The Interpretation of Cultures.* New York: Basic Books.
Geschwind, N., and M. Fusillo
1966   "Color Naming Defects in Association with Alexia." *Arch.
       Neurol.* 15:137–46.
Gibbons, Reginald, ed.
1979   *The Poet's Work: 29 Masters of 20th Century Poetry on the Ori-
       gins and Practice of Their Art.* Boston: Houghton Mifflin. (See
       especially the articles by Mandelstam, Lorca, Stevens, Berry,
       Valéry, Moore, Heaney, and Snyder.)
Gilberti, Maturino
1559   *Diccionario de la lengua tarasca o de Michoacan.* Colección
       Siglo XVI, no. 9. Mexico City (Reprinted, 1901, 1902.)

Gipper, Helmut
  1972 *Gibt es ein sprachliches Relativitätsprinzip? Untersuchungen zur Sapir-Whorf Hypothese.* Frankfurt: S. Fischer. ·
Goodenough, Ward H.
  1956 "Componential Analysis and the Analysis of Meaning." *Language* 32:195–216.
Goodman, Nelson
  1976 *Languages of Art.* Indianapolis: Hackett.
Gossen, Gary
  1974 "To Speak with a Heated Heart: Chamula Canons of Style and Performance." In Baumann and Scherzer, eds., 1974:389–417.
Greenberg, Joseph
  1966 *Language Universales.* The Hague: Mouton.
——, ed.
  1963 *Universals of Language.* Cambridge, Mass.: MIT. (See especially articles by Greenberg, Weinreich, Ullmann, and Jakobson.)
Gross, Harvey
  1979 *The Structure of Verse.* New York: Ecco.
Gumperz, John J.
  1971 *Language in Social Groups.* Stanford: Stanford University Press.
Halpern, Daniel, ed.
  1975 *The American Poetry Anthology.* New York: Doubleday.
Hamp, Eric, Fred W. Householder, and Robert Austerlitz, eds.
  1966 *Readings in Linguistics II.* Chicago: University of Chicago Press.
Hardin, Margaret Ann
  1977 *Structure and Creativity: Family Style in Tarascan Greenware Painting.* 2 vols. Ph.D. dissertation, University of Chicago.
Harris, Zelig S.
  1951 *Methods in Structural Linguistics.* Chicago: University of Chicago Press.
Harrison, Jim
  1982 *Selected and New Poems, 1961–81.* New York: Dell.
Haviland, John
  1977 *Gossip, Reputation, and Knowledge in Zinacantan.* Chicago: University of Chicago Press.
Head, Gwen
  1976 "Stinging Nettle." In *A Geography of Poets,* edited by Edward Field. New York: Bantam.
Heisenberg, Werner
  1958 *Physics and Philosophy.* New York: Harper, Torchbooks.
Henderson, Harold G.
  1958 *An Introduction to Haiku.* New York: Doubleday, Anchor.
Herder, Johann Gottfried von
  1968 *Reflections on the Philosophy of Mankind.* Translated by F. E. Manuels. Chicago: University of Chicago Press.

Hockett, Charles F.
1954 "Chinese versus English: An Exploration of the Whorfian Hypothesis." In Hoijer, ed., 1954:106–127.
1955 *A Manual of Phonology.* Memoir 11, *International Journal of American Linguistics.* Baltimore: Waverly Press.
Hoijer, Harry
1954 "The Sapir-Whorf Hypothesis." In *Language in Culture,* edited by Harry Hoijer, pp. 92–106. Chicago: University of Chicago Press.
Hollander, John
1981 *Rhyme's Reason: A Guide to English Verse.* New Haven: Yale University Press.
Humboldt, Wilhelm von
1971 *Linguistic Variability and Intellectual Development.* Translated by George C. Buck and Frithjof A. Raven. Coral Gables, Fla.: University of Miami Press.
Hunn, Eugene
1975 "Cognitive Processes in Folk Ornithology: The Identification of Gulls." Berkeley: Language-Behavior Research Laboratory, University of California.
Hymes, Dell
1961 "On Typology of Cognitive Styles in Language (with Examples from Chinookan)." *Anthropological Linguistics* 3:22–54.
1974 *Foundations of Sociolinguistics.* Philadelphia: University of Pennsylvania Press.
1981 *In Vain I Tried to Tell You: Essays in Native American Ethnopoetics.* Philadelphia: University of Pennsylvania Press.
——, ed.
1964 *Language in Culture and Society.* With a foreword by A. L. Kroeber. New York: Harper and Row.
Jakobson, Roman
1939 "Signe zero." In Hamp, Householder, and Austerlitz, eds., 1966:109–16.
1956 "Two Aspects of Language and Two Types of Aphasic Disturbance." In *Fundamentals of Language,* by Roman Jakobson and Morris Halle, pp. 55–83. The Hague: Mouton.
1959 "On Linguistic Aspects of Translation." In *On Translation,* by Reuben A. Brower, pp. 232–39. Cambridge, Mass.: Harvard University Press.
1960 "Concluding Statement: Linguistics and Poetics." In Sebeok, ed., 1960:350–78.
1961 "Poezija grammatiki i grammatika poezij." *Poetics/Poetyka.* Warsaw and The Hague.
Jones, Daniel
1957 *An Outline of English Phonetics.* New York: W. Heffer.

Joos, Martin
    1958 "Semiology: A Linguistic Theory of Meaning." *Studies in Linguistics* 13:53–70. Buffalo.
———, ed.
    1957 *Readings in Linguistics I.* Washington, D.C.: American Council of Learned Societies.
Jung, Carl, et al.
    1976 *Man and His Symbols.* New York: Doubleday, Windfall.
Kant, Immanuel
    1949 *The Philosophy of Kant: Immanuel Kant's Moral and Political Writings.* Translated by Carl J. Friedrich. New York: Modern Library.
Kay, Paul, and Willett Kempton
    1984 "What Is the Sapir-Whorf Hypothesis?" *American Anthropologist* 86(1):65–80.
Kay, Paul, and Chad K. McDaniel
    1973 "The Linguistic Significance of Basic Color Terms." *Language* 54(3):610–46.
King, Robert D.
    1969 *Historical Linguistics and Generative Grammar.* Englewood Cliffs, N.J.: Prentice-Hall.
Kiparsky, Paul
    1973 "The Role of Linguistics in a Theory of Poetry." *Daedalus* 102:231–44.
Kochman, Thomas, ed.
    1972 *Rappin' and Stylin' Out: Communication in Urban Black America.* Urbana: University of Illinois Press.
Kroeber, Alfred L.
    1943 "Structure, Function, and Pattern in Biology and Anthropology." *Scientific Monthly* 66:105–13.
Kroeber, Karl
    1983 "The Wolf Comes: Indian Poetry and Linguistic Criticism." In Swann, ed., 1983:98–111.
Labov, William
    1966 "The Social Motivation of a Sound Change." *Word* 19(3):273–309.
    1972 "Rules for Ritual Insults." In Kochman, ed., 1972:265–315.
Ladefoged, Peter
    1971 *Preliminaries to Linguistic Phonetics.* Chicago: University of Chicago Press.
Langer, Suzanne
    1951 *Philosophy in a New Key.* New York: Mentor.
Langley, E. F.
    1915 *The Poetry of Giacomo da Lentino.* Cambridge, Mass.: Harvard University Press.

Lao Tzu

    1978   *Tao Te Ching.* Translated by Gia-Fu Feng and Jane English. New York: Random House. (See also the translations by D. C. Lau, A. Waley, and D. T. Suzuki and Paul Carus.)

Laughlin, Robert M.

    1975   *The Great Tzotzil Dictionary of San Lorenzo Zinacantan.* Washington, D.C.: Smithsonian Institution.

Leech, Geoffrey

    1969   *A Linguistic Guide to English Poetry.* London: Longmans.

Lefebvre, Henri

    1977   "Ideology and the Sociology of Knowledge." In Dolgin, Kemnitzer, and Scheider 1977:254–69.

Lehmann, Winfred P.

    1974   *Proto-Indo-European Syntax.* Austin: University of Texas Press.

Lévi-Strauss, Claude

    1966   *The Savage Mind.* London: Weidenfeld and Nicholson.

    1969   *The Raw and the Cooked.* Translated by John and Doreen Weightman. Harper and Row, Torchbooks.

Lin, Julia C.

    1974   *Modern Chinese Poetry: An Introduction.* Seattle: University of Washington Press.

Linton, Ralph

    1945   *The Science of Man in the World Crisis.* New York: Columbia University Press.

Liu, James

    1974   *The Art of Chinese Poetry.* Chicago: University of Chicago Press.

Lorca, Federico García

    1979   "The Duende: Theory and Divertissement." In Gibbons, ed., 1979:28–42.

Lowie, Robert

    1972   "Association." In Maranda, ed., 1972:32–39.

Lyons, John

    1983   *Semantics,* vol. 2. Cambridge: Cambridge University Press.

McDonnell, Arthur A.

    1971   *A Vedic Grammar for Students.* Bombay: Oxford University Press.

Malinowski, Bronislav

    1923   "The Problem of Meaning in Primitive Languages." In *The Meaning of Meaning,* by C. K. Ogden and I. A. Richards, pp. 451–510. London: Kegan Paul.

Mandelstam, Osip

    1983   *Selected Poems.* Translated by Clarence Brown and W. S. Merwin. New York: Atheneum.

Maranda, Pierre, ed.
  1972 *Mythology.* Baltimore: Penguin. (See especially articles by
     Cassirer, Lowie, Propp, and Lévi-Strauss.)
Marx, Karl
  1977 "The Fetishism of Commodities and the Secret Thereof." In
     Dolgin, Kemnitzer, and Scheider 1977:245–53.
Marx, Karl, and Friedrich Engels
  1959 *Marx and Engels.* Edited by Lewis S. Feuer. New York:
     Doubleday, Anchor.
Mathesius, Vilem
  1964 "On the Potentiality of the Phenomena of Language." In Vachek,
     ed., 1964:1–33.
Mathiot, Madeleine
  1964 "Noun Classes and Folk Taxonomy in Papago." In Hymes, ed.,
     1964:161–67.
Melville, Herman
  1967 *Moby-Dick.* Edited by Harrison Hayford and Herschel Parker.
     New York: W. W. Norton. (Chapter 42, "The Whiteness of the
     Whale," reprinted in Dolgin, Kemnitzer, and Scheider, eds.,
     1977.)
Merleau-Ponty, Maurice
  1964 *The Primacy of Perception.* Evanston, Ill.: Northwestern Uni-
     versity Press.
Miller, George A.
  1956 "The Magical Number Seven, Plus or Minus Two: Some Limits
     on Our Capacity for Processing Information." *Psychological Re-
     view* 63:81–97.
Mönch, Walter
  1955 *Das Sonett: Gestalt und Geschichte.* Heidelberg: F. H. Kerle.
Monod, Jacques
  1972 *Chance and Necessity.* New York: Random House, Vintage
     Books.
Moore, Marianne
  1979 "Idiosyncrasy and Technique." In Gibbons, ed., 1979:215–30.
Morris, Christopher
  1982 *Deconstruction: Theory and Practice.* London and New York:
     Methuen.
Muhařovský, Ian
  1964 "Standard Language and Poetic Language." In Garvin, ed.,
     1964:17–31.
  1966 "La phonologie et la poetique." In Hamp, Householder, and
     Austerlitz, eds., 1966:6–14.
Musil, Alois
  1928 *The Manners and Customs of the Rwalla Bedouins.* Oriental
     Studies and Explorations, No. 6. New York: American Geo-
     graphical Society.

Nabokov, Vladimir
1981 "The 'Eugene Onegin' Stanza." In *Eugene Onegin*, 1:9–14. Princeton: Princeton University Press.
Nagler, Michael N.
1974 *Spontaneity and Tradition: A Study in the Oral Art of Homer.* Berkeley: University of California Press.
Neumann, Erich
1972 *The Great Mother: An Analysis of the Archetype.* Princeton: Princeton University Press.
Newman, Stanley, and Ann Gayton
1964 "Yokuts Narrative Style." In Hymes, ed., 1964: 372–81.
Nietzsche, Friedrich
1967 *The Birth of Tragedy* and *The Case of Wagner*. Translated by Walter Kaufman. New York: Random House, Vintage Books.
1981 *A Nietzsche Reader*. Translated by J. Hollingdale. New York: Penguin.
Ohmann, Richard
1964 "Generative Grammars and the Concept of Literary Style." *Word* 20: 423–39.
Olshewsky, Thomas, ed.
1969 *Problems in the Philosophy of Language.* New York: Holt, Rinehart and Winston. (See especially articles by Peirce, Cassirer, Linsky, Kant, Quine, Winter, and Black.)
Ornstein, Robert, ed.
1973 *The Nature of Human Consciousness.* San Francisco: W. H. Freeman.
Packard, William
1974 *The Craft of Poetry.* New York: Doubleday.
Parry, Milman
1971 *The Making of Homeric Verse: The Collected Papers of Milman Parry.* Edited by Adam Parry. Oxford: Clarendon Press.
Pascal, Blaise
1979 *Pensées.* Translated by A. J. Krailsheimer. New York: Penguin.
Peirce, Charles S.
1958 *Charles S. Peirce: Selected Writings.* Edited by P. P. Wiener. New York: Dover.
Penn, Julia
1972 *Linguistic Relativity versus Innate Ideas: The Origin of the Sapir-Whorf Hypothesis in German Thought.* The Hague: Mouton.
Peristiany, J. G.
1966 *Honor and Shame: The Values of a Mediterranean Society.* Chicago: University of Chicago Press.
Preminger, Alex, Franke J. Warnke, and O. B. Hardison
1974 *Princeton Encyclopedia of Poetry and Poetics.* Princeton: Princeton University Press.

Pushkin, Alexander
   1981 *Eugene Onegin*. Translated by Walter Arndt. New York: Dutton.
Raine, Kathleen
   1967 *Defending Ancient Springs*. Oxford: Oxford University Press.
Ramanujan, A. K.
   1967 *The Interior Landscape: Love Poems from a Classical Tamil Anthology*. Bloomington: University of Indiana Press.
Reichard, Gladys
   1963 *Navaho Religion: A Study of Symbolism*. New York: Pantheon.
Renou, Louis
   1952 *Grammaire de la langue védique*. Lyon/Paris: IAC.
Ricoeur, Paul
   1973 "Philosophy and Religious Language." *Journal of Religion* 54:71–84.
Rosaldo, Michelle
   1972 "Metaphors and Folk Classification." *Southwestern Journal of Anthropology* 28:83–98.
Rothenberg, Jerome
   1969 *Technicians of the Sacred*. New York: Doubleday, Anchor.
Sahlins, Marshall
   1977 "Colors and Cultures." In Dolgin, Kemnitzer, and Scheider, eds., 1977:165–83.
Samarin, William J.
   1970 "Inventory and Word Choice in Expressive Language." *Word* 26(2):153–69.
Sapir, David J., and J. Christopher Crocker
   1977 *The Social Use of Metaphor: Essays in the Anthropology of Rhetoric*. Philadelphia: University of Pennsylvania Press. (See especially D. J. Sapir's "The Anatomy of Metaphor.")
Sapir, Edward
   1907 "Herder's *Ursprung der Sprache*." *Modern Philology* 5:109–42.
   1921a *Language*. New York: Harcourt, Brace.
   1921b "The Musical Foundations of Verse." *Journal of English and Germanic Philology* 20:213–38.
   1925 "Emily Dickinson, a Primitive." Review of *The Complete Poems of Emily Dickinson*, and *The Life and Letters of Emily Dickinson*, by M. D. Bianchi. *Poetry* 26:97–105.
   1951 *The Selected Writings of Edward Sapir*. Edited by David G. Mandelbaum. Berkeley and Los Angeles: University of California Press. (See especially articles on phonology, literature, and personality.)
Saussure, Ferdinand de
   1959 *Course in General Linguistics*. Edited by C. Balley and A. Sechehaye; translated by Wade Baskin. New York: Philosophical Library.

Saville-Troike, Muriel, ed.
> 1977 *Linguistics and Anthropology: Georgetown University Round-table on Languages and Linguistics.* Georgetown: Georgetown University Press. (See especially articles by Brown, McLendon, and Silverstein.)

Schneider, David M.
> 1965 "Some Muddles in the Models, or, How the System Really Works." In *The Relevance of Models for Social Anthropology,* edited by Michael Banton. London: Tavistock.

Scully, James
> 1965 *Modern Poetics.* New York: McGraw-Hill.

Sebeok, Thomas, ed.
> 1960 *Style in Language.* Cambridge, Mass.: MIT.
> 1964 *Approaches to Semiotics.* The Hague: Mouton.
> 1979 *A Perfusion of Signs.* Bloomington: University of Indiana Press.

Sherzer, Joel
> 1983 *Kuna Ways of Speaking: An Ethnographic Perspective.* Austin: University of Texas Press.

Simpson, George G.
> 1955 *The Meaning of Evolution.* New York: Mentor.

Slotkin, Richard
> 1973 "Moby-Dick: The American National Epic." In *Regeneration through Violence: The Mythology of the American Frontier, 1600–1860,* pp. 539–550. Middletown, Conn.: Wesleyan University Press.

Snyder, Gary
> 1973 "Poetry and the Primitive." In Allen and Tallman, eds., 1973:395–407.
> 1978 *Myths and Texts.* New York: New Directions.
> 1979 "The Real Work." In Gibbons, ed., 1979:283–97.

Sorokin, Pitrim
> 1947 *Society, Culture, and Personality.* New York: Harper.

Stankiewicz, Edward
> 1958 "Slavic Kinship and the Perils of the Soul." *Journal of American Folklore* 71:115–22.
> 1979 "Poetics and Verbal Art." In Sebeok, ed., 1979:54–77.

Steinberg, Danny D., and Leon A. Jakobovits, eds.
> 1974 *Semantics.* Cambridge: Cambridge University Press.

Stenbock-Fermor, Elizabeth
> 1975 *The Architecture of Anna Karenina: A History of Writing, Structure, and Message.* Lisse: Peter de Ridder.

Stevens, Wallace
> 1951a *The Necessary Angel: Essays on Reality and the Imagination.* New York: Alfred A. Knopf.

1951b   *The Collected Poems of Wallace Stevens.* New York: Alfred
A. Knopf.
1977   *Opus Posthumous: Poems; Plays, Prose.* Edited by Samuel
French Morse. New York: Alfred A. Knopf.

Swadesh, Morris
1969   *Elementos del tarasco antiguo.* Mexico City: Universidad Na-
cional Autónoma de México.

Swann, Bryan, ed.
1983   *Smoothing the Ground: Essays on Native American Oral Literature.* Berkeley: University of California Press.

Tambiah, Stanley
1968   "The Magical Power of Words." Malinowski Memorial Lecture.
Man 3:175–208.

Tannen, Deborah, ed.
1982   *Spoken and Written Language: Exploring Orality and Literacy.*
Vol. 9 of *Advances in Discourse Processes,* edited by Roy O.
Freedle. Norwood, N.J.: Ablex.
1984   *Conversational Style: Analyzing Talk among Friends.* Norwood, N.J.: Ablex.

Tedlock, Dennis
1978   *Finding the Center: Narrative Poetry of the Zuni Indians
Translated from Performances in Zuni by Andrew Peynetsa
and Walter Sanchez.* Lincoln: University of Nebraska Press.
1983   *The Spoken Word and the Work of Interpretation.* Philadelphia:
University of Pennsylvania Press.

Todorov, Tsvetan
1977   *The Poetics of Prose.* Translated by Richard Howard. Ithaca:
Cornell University Press.

Tolstoy, Leo
1925   *What Is Art?* and *Essays on Art.* Translated by Aylmer Maude.
London:
1966   *War and Peace: The Maude Translation; Backgrounds and
Sources; Essays in Criticism.* Edited by George Gibians. New
York: W. W. Norton.

Traugott, Elizabeth, and Mary L. Pratt
1980   *Linguistics for Students of Literature.* New York: Harcourt,
Brace, Jovanovich.

Turner, Victor
1966   "Color Classification in Ndembu Ritual." In *Anthropological
Approaches to the Study of Religion,* edited by Michael Banton.
London: Tavistock.
1967   *The Forest of Symbols.* Ithaca: Cornell University Press.
1969   *The Ritual Process: Structure and Anti-structure.* Chicago:
Aldine.

1977 "Symbols in African Ritual." In Dolgin, Kemnitzer, and Scheider, eds., 1977:183–95.

Tyler, Steven
1978 *The Said and the Unsaid.* New York: Academic Press.

Untermeyer, Louis, ed.
1942 *A Treasury of Great Poems.* New York: Simon and Schuster.

Vachek, Josef, ed.
1964 *A Prague School Reader in Linguistics.* Bloomington: University of Indiana Press.

Voegelin, Carl, and Florence M. Voegelin
1957 *Hopi Domains: A Lexical Approach to the Problem of Selection.* Memoir 14, *International Journal of American Linguistics.*

Wagner, Roy
1975 *The Invention of Culture.* Englewood Cliffs, N.J.: Prentice-Hall.

Wallace, Anthony F. C.
1956 "Mazeway Resynthesis: A Biocultural Theory of Religious Inspiration." *Transactions of the New York Academy of Sciences,* ser. 2, 18(7):626–38.

Weinreich, Uriel
1963 "On the Semantic Structure of Language." In Greenberg, ed., 1963:142–217.
1974 "Explorations in Semantic Theory." In Steinberg and Jakobovits, eds., 1974:308–29.

West, Robert C.
1984 *Cultural Geography of the Modern Tarascan Area.* Smithsonian Institution, Institute of Social Anthropology, Pub. 7. Washington, D.C.: Government Printing Office.

Whitehead, Alfred N.
1933 *Adventures of Ideas.* New York: The Free Press. (See especially chapters 17 and 18.)
1948 *Science and the Modern World.* New York: New American Library, Pelican.

Whitman, Cedric H.
1965 *Homer and the Homeric Tradition.* New York: W. W. Norton.

Whorf, Benjamin Lee
1964 *Language, Thought, and Reality.* Edited by John Carroll. Cambridge, Mass.: MIT.

Winner, Ellen
1982 *Invented Worlds: The Psychology of the Arts.* Cambridge, Mass.: Harvard University Press.

Wittgenstein, Ludwig
1953 *Philosophical Investigations.* Translated by G. E. M. Anscombe. Oxford: Blackwell.

1958   *The Blue and Brown Books.* New York: Harper, Torchbooks.
1978   *Remarks on Color.* Berkeley: University of California Press.
Wordsworth, William
1984   "Peter Bell, A Tale." In *The Poetical Works of William Words-worth,* p. 97. Oxford Author Series. Oxford: Oxford University Press.
Wyatt, Sir Thomas
1975   *Collected Poems.* Edited by Joost Daalder. Oxford: Oxford University Press.

Permission Notices

Index of Names and Titles

Subject Index

aesthetics, 9, 11, 17, 22, 54
African: language, 36; literature, 32; proverbs, 44
algorithms, 122, 126, 136, 138, 140
alienation, 2, 39, 66–67
American: English, 6, 16, 32, 51, 100, 106; poetry, 27, 51, 92, 101, 103, 155–56; symbol, 161; traditions, 107; values, 105. *See also* Indian, American
analogy, 4, 29, 30, 134, 136, 144–45
anthropology, 1, 9, 10, 12, 66–67, 127, 134, 139, 160; and linguistics, 5–7, 13, 16, 137–38, 147
aphasia, 57, 107, 134, 145
Arabic, 27, 72, 86–87
art, 10–12, 41, 53, 70, 81, 146, 155, 158–60
aspect (grammatical), 32, 45, 144
associations, 20, 30, 127, 146; and dreams, 72, 75–76
Aztec, 135

baseball, 19, 22, 24–25, 37, 41, 105, 107–10
beauty, 3, 16, 17, 21–22, 70, 77, 160
Bedouin, 27
behavior, 13, 15, 120–22
Bengali, 84, 162
biology, 80, 121, 131, 132, 134, 145
Black defiance, 103
Black English, 25
body (human), 2, 47–48, 136, 175
brain, 6, 30, 118, 142
British, 16, 141

chaos, 4, 6, 7, 54–55, 105, 107, 117–72
chiasmus, 40, 78, 79, 90
"Chicano," 134
child language, 15, 54, 154
Chinese, 26, 27, 32, 45, 51, 53, 124–25, 128–29, 141
code, 20, 34, 39, 127, 129, 137, 145